WEEKEND**escape**

A great weekend
in London

A major destination for many intercontinental airlines and just a few hours by train from the heart of Europe, how can one resist the appeal of London? The capital of Great Britain has never been so close to the rest of Europe, and it remains wickedly tempting. London is perhaps the only city in Europe which combines with apparent harmony both the traditions of a bygone age and a certain cozy elegance with the most outrageous fashions and over-the-top clubs – the envy of the whole world.

Whether you are seeking that quality cashmere, a raincoat that won't go out of fashion or a pair of platform shoes; whether you dream of the splendor of all things royal or whether you would not wish to be seen anywhere but at the most fashionable nightclubs, you soon come to realize that London is just for you. Windows overflowing with Western abundance, London's boutiques and department stores offer a wide variety, suited to all tastes and budgets. The different ethnic communities have further enriched this vast emporium with their particular wares; it is virtually a world shopping tour that awaits you just a few hours away from home.

th six million inhabitants d an area four times the e of Paris, London esents a thousand faces: own, chic or mocking, which those of the former untries of the Empire have en superimposed. In ndon you will find a mpletely unique street etry, one where the clouds Turner's paintings are

to pronounce judgment or even express surprise. It is only the tourists who turn around to look again at the sight of a shaven-haired couple passing, with noses, lips and ears pierced. Londoners perhaps permit themselves this independence of spirit and indifference to appearances not because they are slaves to fashion

creative dynamism, and the economic crises the country has faced have only served to stimulate its creativity. Like a strange planet where gloominess is banished, this city is the best destination there is for a morale boost. Lift your inhibitions, forget your prejudices and allow yourself to be surprised by all the eccentricities. You are in London and you will be amazed at the feeling of liberty to be found. You can spend a sleepless weekend

produced in the puddles n the sidewalk. Around one reet corner the smell of ying onions and a man in turban will give you the rief impression of being in ombay, just as you're alking out of Marks & pencer. Passing by you night see a group of cotsmen in kilts, a young oman with pink hair half naved off, a host of yuppies om the City complete with ree-piece suits and cell hones, a Miss Marple in a vinset, a lady from the West nd carrying her shoes in er hands so as to enjoy the eel of the grass in Hyde Park nder her feet... All these tyles, all these looks exist ide by side with a sovereign ndifference. No one seems

but because they are creating it on a daily basis. Their inventions, cobbled together with imagination and resourcefulness, are today copied in showrooms and on podiums throughout the fashion world. It is to this permanent ebullience that London owes its

here, you will leave determined to come back, and you *will* return very soon.

Practicalities

When is best?

Climate

No, it does not rain all the time in London; in winter it also happens to snow occasionally! Statistically, it rains only every other day. July is the sunniest month, or the least wet, it is for you to see for yourself, but the temperatures remain mild during the winter, rarely falling below freezing.

How to get there

How you arrive in London will probably depend on whether the city is the starting point of your trip or part of a wider European trip. If coming directly from North America, you will certainly be arriving by plane. If coming from other parts of continental Europe, particulaly France,

the train and boat are also options.

By plane

US airlines

Amost all of the US airlines offer regular direct flights to London, sometimes several times a day.

American Airlines:
☎ (800) 433 7300
www.aa.com

Delta:
☎ (800) 221 1212
www.delta.com

Northwest:
☎ (800) 447 4747
www.nwa.com

US Airways:
☎ (800) 428 4322
www.usairways.com

There are many special offers, but these usually require you to fly at specified times or dates.

British airways
☎ (800) 247 9297
www.british-airways.com
British Airways is the UK's largest carrier. Regular flights arrive in London from most major North Atlantic cities.

Virgin Atlantic
☎ (800) 821 5438
www.virgin-atlantic.com
British Airways' major rival across the Altantic with regular flights to New York, Boston, Detroit, Fort Lauderdale, Houston, Las Vegas, Los Angeles, Miami, New York, Orlando, Philadelphia, San Francisco and Washington, as well as major Canadian cities.

Other international airlines
You can often find flights to other European cities with a London stopover:

Air France:
☎ (800) 237 2747
www.airfrance.com

KLM:
☎ (800) 447 4747
www.klm.com

Lufthansa:
☎ (800) 563 5954
www.lufthansa.com

By train

Eurostar
www.eurostar.com
The high-speed Eurostar takes 2 hours 35 minutes from Paris and 2 hours from Lille to reach Waterloo Station. Waterloo is located close to the heart of the city center, a few minutes by subway from the liveliest districts, such as Leicester Square. When you consider transfer times between airports and the city center, and the almost inevitable delays surrounding flights, it is much easier and more relaxing to travel by train if you are using France as a base for a European trip. (Prices are approximately the same whether by plane or train.) Eurostar regularly offers weekend deals. Depending on the date and if making reservations in advance, it is possible to obtain second-class round-trip tickets for around £90.

FROM THE AIRPORT TO THE CENTER OF LONDON

From Heathrow
The simplest method is to take the subway. The Piccadilly Line, which runs every five or ten minutes, will take you to the center of London in 50 minutes. It stops at Piccadilly Circus, Leicester Square and Covent Garden. There is also a bus service which will take you either to Victoria Station (line A1) or to Euston and Russell Square (line A2), but it takes one and a half hours and only leaves every 30 minutes.

From Gatwick
Take the Gatwick Express train, which leaves every 15 or 30 minutes and will bring you to Victoria Station in half an hour.

Taxis are available from both airports, but the trip is very expensive (between £40 and £60) and you will not gain very much time when you consider the distance and the delays. Under no circumstances should you be tempted to use an unlicensed taxi, otherwise you may get an unpleasant surprise when it comes to paying the fare for the trip.

It is necessary to stay overnight on Saturday in order to obtain weekend rates. Tickets cannot always be exchanged, and rarely reimbursed. Make inquiries before purchasing your tickets.

By Boat

If you're being more ambitious and touring in a car, you can consider coming to the UK by ferry.

P&O

www.poferries.com
This company also offers ferry + bus or train deals at very competitive prices. Routes: Calais – Dover and Le Havre – Portsmouth.

Brittany Ferries

www.brittany-ferries.com
Routes: Roscoff – Plymouth, Saint-Malo – Portsmouth, Cherbourg – Poole, Caen – Portsmouth.

Sea France-Sealink

www.seafrance.com
Route: Calais – Dover.

Hoverspeed

www.hoverspeed.com
Routes: Calais – Dover, Boulogne – Folkestone, Dieppe – Newhaven.

Car rental

Although the international car rental companies are well represented at all London airports, driving into the city itself is not recommended. Apart from the size of the city, difficulties of driving on the left and very expensive parking fees, a tax is payable (the congestion charge) to drive in the city center, an area bordered by Victoria Station, King's Cross, Tower Bridge and Elephant and Castle (approx. 21 sq. km/8 sq. miles). This tax is £8 per day and applies between Monday and Friday, 7am to 6.30pm (except public holidays) at entry points. It is possible to pay by Internet, by telephone, by SMS or by mail.
☎ 0845 900 12 34
www. cclondon.com

Visas

EU citizens should carry a valid ID card or passport. Non-EU citizens will require a valid passport, although US citizens do not require a visa to enter the UK for tourist visits of less than six months. You do, however, need enough money to support yourself for your planned stay. No vaccinations are required.

Exchange and budgeting

The English currency is the pound sterling (£), made up of 100 pence (singular: one penny). Denominations are as follows: bills of £5, £10, £20 and £50, and coins of £1 and £2, as well as of 1, 2, 5, 10, 20 and 50 pence. You may take as much currency as you wish, but you will have to make a customs declaration for more than £5,000. It is preferable to change currency before you leave.

Customs

r travelers returning to other J countries, there are few strictions on alcohol or bacco products. The only pulation is that the goods ust be for personal use and iidelines are provided, for ample 10 liters of spirits,) liters of wine and 800 garettes.

ity-free limits for travelers aving the EU are as follows:
cohol over 22%: 1L *or*
cohol not over 22%: 2L *and*
ill table wine: 2L
igarettes: 200 *or* cigars: 50 *or*
obacco: 250gm
erfume: 60ml
oilet water: 250ml.

bove all do not bring in any efensive weapon such as tear-as; you will be subject to a eavy fine. Almost all firearms re banned in Great Britain; nly personal alarms are ermitted.

Insurance

f you pay for your ticket by redit card, you automatically enefit from some insurance egarding your luggage, the ossible cancellation of your rip and medical repatriation. ind out more from your credit card company or ask your bank. EU citizens can also reclaim potential health costs. Non-EU citizens should make sure they have adequate cover. The cost is low but it offers real benefits in case of problems.

SOME USEFUL ADDRESSES

Great Britain Tourist Office
Email: gbinfo@visitbritain.org
www.visitbritain.com
The official tourist organization with links to many other useful sites.

British embassies overseas
US: 3100 Massachusetts Avenue NW, Washington DC 2008
☎ 01 46 33 16 24
www.britainusa.com

Canada:High Commission, 80 Elgin Street, Ottowa 5K7
☎ 613 2371530

Ireland: 29 Merrion Road, Ballsbridge, Dublin 4
☎ 01 203 700
www.britishembassy.ie

Australia: High Commission, Commonwealth Avenue, Yarralumla, Canberra ACT 2600
☎ 026 270 6666
www.uk.emb.gov.au

New Zealand: High Commission, 44 Hill Street, Wellington 1
☎ 04 472 6049
www.britain.org.nz

South Africa:High Commission, 91 Parliament Street, Cape Town 8001
☎ 21 461 7220

English banks are usually closed at weekends and bureaus de change offer very unfavorable rates. Above all, insure that you have enough money on arrival at the airport or station. You will need it for your transfer to the city and you won't have to waste an often long time waiting in line at the bureau de change. However, there are ATMs available almost everywhere, and it only takes a few minutes to make a withdrawal with your debit or credit card.

Traveler's checks are the best choice for carrying large sums of money. To avoid excess charges, have them in large denominations and if possible exchange them at a branch of the issuing organization. No one could argue that London is a budget destination and currency fluctuations can make this worse. You will probably require between £200 and £400 per person for the weekend, to cover accommodations, meals and transportation. This is, however, the ideal time for

shopping. Clothing, personal effects and accessories are at very attractive prices, and you'll get the distinct impression your trip will be paid for from the savings made. Anyway, that's the kind of argument you'll need to ease your conscience.

What to take

You may find the following checklist useful, but if you forget or need to replace any items, there's every chance that you'll be able to find its equivalent in London.
• A selection of clothing for a wide range of weather conditions. Rainwear is essential all year. Umbrellas are useful but can be more trouble than they're worth, especially on windy days; a lightweight waterproof jacket can be a better option.
• Addresses and phone numbers of emergency contacts.

SALES

These take place in January to February and June to July. It's a good idea to get there early as they are very popular, especially those of the department stores which offer huge discounts. However, many other stores make special offers of varying degrees throughout the year. Watch out for "Sale" stickers in the windows.

HEALTH

If you are taking a course of medication at the time of your departure, do not forget to take with you enough supplies as you are not guaranteed to find the exact equivalent when you arrive. Your prescription could be useful at customs to justify carrying these. If you are an EU citizen make sure you have with you a European Health Insurance Card (EHIC; forms from post offices). This allows you to claim back any medical expenses you may incur while in Great Britain. In any case, all citizens and residents of EU member countries benefit from free health and dental care under the National Health Service in case of emergency. Just be sure to go to an NHS doctor or hospital.

Compass (useful for finding our way).

Driver's license (if you hold license or permit from ustralia, Canada, Ireland, ew Zealand or the USA) or nternational Driver's License f your license is in a anguage other than English).

Photocopies of passport and ravel insurance (or send canned versions of these to an mail account that you can ccess while you are away).

Credit cards (preferably nore than one credit card) nd/or travelers' checks, and a mall amount of sterling cash).

Numbers of credit/debit ards, registration

numbers of cell phones, cameras and other expensive equipment (in case you need to report loss to the police). Keep these separate from the items.

• Spare passport photos for travel cards.

Local time

Britain lies on the famous Greenwich Meridian. Between October and March Britain is on Greenwich Mean Time (GMT). From the thrid Sunday in March until the fourth Sunday in October is the period known as British Summer Time when clocks are one hour ahead of GMT. Times in the US and Canada vary from GMT minus 5 hours to minus 10 hours. Most flights from North America travel overnight and arrive in London early the next morning, losing you several hours along the way.

Voltage

The current in Britain is 240 volts, and North American appliances cannot be used in British sockets. Be sure to take an adapter, or purchase one at the airport, without which your razor or your hair-dryer will have to stay at the bottom of your suitcase.

The jewels
in the crown

Ever since the end of the English Civil War in 1649, Great Britain has lived under a parliamentary monarchy, which means that the sovereign only has a representative power. It is perhaps for this reason that the members of the Royal family remain forever popular in British hearts and minds. You'll be able to gauge this for yourself by simply watching one of their ceremonies.

The Royals:
A crown in peril?

Only a few years ago, the future of the Windsor family was in some doubt. The

affairs of the Crown were the object of innumerable disclosures, with stories appearing in the UK's newspapers, such as *The Sun*. Indeed, their very existence was called into question after the death of Lady Diana. Since then, the advisers to the Royal family have worked hard to improve the image of the Crown. This task has been made easier by the coming of age of Prince William and Prince Harry, who are taking well to their public roles. The country's opinion of the Royals improved enough to

allow Prince Charles to finally marry Camilla, who became the Duchess of Cornwall in April 2005.

Royal fortune and misfortune

The three largest diamonds in the world, two-thirds of all the known paintings by Leonardo da Vinci, an income estimated at 300 million pounds – the Queen of England is hardly impoverished but, since April 1994, her fortune has been subject to taxation just like that of any one of her subjects. The civil list (the annual budget allocated to her) amounts to only 25 pence per inhabitant; however, more and more of the English consider this to be too much. More than half of them predict that the British monarchy will not survive

beyond the year 2050.

God save the Queen!

Ever since 1066, Westminster Abbey has marked the greatest events in the life of the sovereign. During the coronation, he or she enters the Abbey and sits upon the throne of Edward the Confessor," which dates from the 15th century. The Archbishop of Canterbury presents the sovereign with the symbols of power: first the sword, then the royal mantle, the crown, the scepter – which

holds one of the largest diamonds in the world (the Star of Africa) – the orb (surmounted by a cross) which symbolizes the power of Christ on earth, and the seal of the sovereign ornamented with the cross of St. George, in other words the British ensign picked out in sapphires and rubies. All of these accoutrements signify the role of the monarch, head of the state and of the Anglican Church. You can admire them at the Tower of London (see p. 68). The coronation of Elizabeth II in 1953 was the first such occasion to be broadcast on television and so you could say it was downhill from there.

The Changing of the Guard

The Changing of the Guard takes place, complete with fanfare, every day at 11.30am from April to September, and every other day from October to March, except when it is raining. Instead of standing in front of Buckingham Palace, from where you won't see much, go rather to the front of the Horse Guards building in Whitehall, where the same ceremony takes place at 11.00am Mondays through Saturdays and at 10.00am on Sundays, with far fewer people around.

THE CEREMONY OF THE KEYS

You have two options for seeing the Ceremony of the Keys at the Tower of London. Either you can purchase a ticket on the day at the door, or simply content yourself with observing from outside. This ceremony, almost seven centuries old, only lasts for seven minutes, but it is truly fascinating since it is possible to sense the weight of attachment to tradition. Everything begins at 9.30pm. The Chief Yeoman Warder and his escort, dressed in black and red Tudor costumes, arrive in order to lock the front gate by the light of a lantern. They then lock all the other gates of the Tower. During their passage the keys are saluted by the sentinels, and the Chief Warder concludes with the traditional salute to the Queen. Very seldom attended, particularly when it is already dark, this is more intimate and mysterious than the Changing of the Guard where the tourists crowd around.

London
at the end
of the Baroque era

The Black Death and the Great Fire of London were the most spectacular occurrences of this period, which led to an intense phase of reconstruction. It was in this troubled climate that Christopher Wren was charged with restoring the devastated areas and entrusted with the construction of several churches in the city, such as the famous St. Paul's Cathedral.

ideal conditions fostering the risk of fire. Dwellings were often overcrowded, badly aired and notable for an almost entire absence of sanitation. In this context, it is easy to understand the ravages caused by epidemics such as the plague of 1665 which claimed almost 70,000 victims.

Political upheaval

At the same time as the large-scale modifications of London's urban infrastructure there came a turning-point in the country's history. Between 1642, the date of Charles I's execution and Cromwell's accession to power, and 1688, when William of Orange was installed upon the throne, England lived under a regime of parliamentary democracy which soon became the model for an enlightened Europe. These ups and downs

did not hold back the development of the economy, the prosperity of the middle classes or the growth of the capital.

Medieval city planning and sanitation

Urban development often took place among anarchic conditions following the inherited procedures of the Middle Ages; houses were constructed entirely of wood and ranged one beside the other along narrow streets,

The monument to the Great Fire of London in the City

...ne thing after ...nother

...sfortunes always come in ...os. In the following year, ...66, occurred the Great Fire ...London which ravaged the ...y for five days and five ...ghts, causing the destruction ...13,000 homes and 89 ...urches: in other words ...most the entire original

city and rid it of the last bacilli of the plague.

From a clean sweep to reconstruction

Profiting from this enforced "clean sweep," municipal regulations were adopted with a view toward reconstruction. The Building Act of 1667, for example, stipulated a

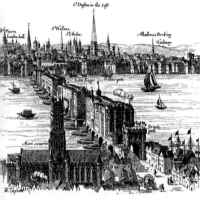

...nter of London. ...e area upon which this ...saster fell corresponds to the ...odern City of London. ...he fire probably began in ...bakery oven, but at the ...me rumors of a papist plot ...arried much weight and ...en provoked reprisals ...gainst the Catholics. ...t every cloud has a silver ...ning; the Fire sanitized the

minimum road width of 6m (18ft) and forbade the use of wood in the construction of dwellings in favor of bricks. These measures were nevertheless insufficient to constitute a truly coherent plan for reconstruction, and the aristocracy deserted the area, which had only just been rebuilt, in favor of the suburbs to the west: the West End.

KEEP CLEAR TURNING BAY

DONT EVEN THINK OF PARKING HERE

Even rebuilt, the urban fabric of the City reproduced the ancient medieval outline, and the taxi drivers of today no doubt regret that Christopher Wren wasn't given greater resources to lay the foundations for a modern city.

The churches of the City

It was in the City that the architect Christopher Wren built the largest number of churches, centered on the new St. Paul's Cathedral (see p. 68). The majority of these monuments were constructed out of Portland stone, clearly in order to create a contrast with the red brick of neighboring buildings. Full of imagination, Wren adopted very varied designs, often drawing inspiration from Roman examples. His construction sites required considerable sums of money, and a new tax was levied on charcoal in order to finance his reconstruction.

Christopher Wren

CHRISTOPHER WREN (1632–1723)

Nothing in particular recommended Christopher Wren for the reconstruction of London after the Great Fire. His education had been no better than that of his contemporaries, in other words based essentially on apprenticeships in mathematics and medicine. He was, however, principal architect to King Charles II, who was on the throne at that time, and the sovereign entrusted the work to him. Ambitious and visionary, Wren may have hoped to redesign the entire city with wide avenues encircling monumental squares, but this project was considered too expensive and was abandoned.

London
toward 2020

London is undoubtedly the European capital displaying the most creative dynamism. Most trends at the beginning of the new century have been launched from here. This driving force can be found in fashion, music, art, design and, above all, on the street. To visit London is also to witness the birth of the avant-garde and to discover what will be successful in Paris, Rome or Berlin six months, or even ten years, from now.

Vivienne Westwood: avant-garde overtaken by success

This one-time founder member of the punk movement originally created designs for the Sex Pistols; later she became one of the most famous English fashion designers. Today, the elegantly clad are fighting each other to wear her eccentric creations, her bodices and her jackets. She has to some extent been influenced by good taste and conformity, but remains full of inventiveness.

Designers for fashion victims

In the city you'll find the greatest variety of different looks, from the most classic to the most improbable. Even if a uniform must still be worn in school, on the street there is a much greater freedom. London's eccentricity is fed by a multitude of more or less well-recognized designers such as Oward Gasten or Hussein Chalayan as well as by the greats such as Katherine Hamnett and John Galliano.

The laboratory of modern architecture

Squarely facing the City, London's Docklands is little by little becoming a new economic and cultural pole. The often very audacious architectural real estate is proliferating and the whole area is coming to life thanks to the presence of numerous artists who organize festivals and exhibitions. There are lots of very hip restaurants and boutiques.

The triumph of techno

Techno, a musical genre which appeared in 1989, received a triumphal welcome in London. Every weekend the world's best DJs play in the multitude of clubs which the city embraces, those such as the famous Ministry of Sound (see p. 139).

Notions of grandeur

The British celebrated the year 2000 in style. Of the festivities, only a few can still be seen. If the Dome only stayed open for one year, the Millennium Bridge, a pedestrian walkway of a futuristic design, and the London Eye, a Ferris wheel 135m (440ft) high, are the incomparable remains of that celebration of the millennium.

Graphic design and new magazines

Publicity and the press in England, regularly awarded international prizes, are in fact the best in the world. To convince yourself, look at the posters in the subway or leaf through some magazines. The best known are *ID*, *Dazed and Confused* and *The Face*, or the artistic *Frieze*.

Articles for tomorrow

It was in London that the first museum totally dedicated to industrial design was opened, the Design Museum. This is not surprising: English design is most original and certainly not limited only to luxury products, but applies itself also to articles of daily life, something which makes it very accessible. Seek out for example the work of Ron Arad.

A dynamic artistic scene

Since the appearance of what was called the "new English sculpture" in the early 1980s, the London artistic scene has not ceased to reanimate itself. This can be observed in art galleries and museums as well as in alternative venues (non-commercial). Look out for the turbulent Damien Hirst, visual artist and video director, and Turner prize-winner in 1995.

AND SO MANY LITTLE HOLES…

Piercing involves rings, small metal bars or points which can be fixed into various parts of the body, such as eyebrows and navels. This practice has replaced that of tattooing among the most eccentric (and least delicate). You will be struck by its frequency. Much in vogue among the most individualistic, it is slowly spreading to all spheres.

Lord Brummell's
British touch

Arbiter of elegance in the 19th century, this famous dandy has left his imprint on London fashion. Admittedly, tailors' prices are often on the same level as their reputations, but here luxury is never without quality. The best addresses abound and at least one of them must find its way onto your itinerary.

detachable lining, most Barbours come in three-quarter length. In order to extend its lifetime, it is worth an annual waxing with a special preparation purchased separately.

Barbour: waxed cotton ready to wear

Since 1890, the reputation of these waxed cotton jackets has been second to none. Totally waterproof, they were originally hunting or riding jackets, but their chic and unassuming style allows them to replace the traditional raincoat to great advantage, over a suit, for example. Spruce green in color, with a brown corduroy collar and occasionally a

Measure for measure

In London, tailors are not the "two weights, two sizes" variety. By contrast, they voluntarily adopt the half-measure: Once the size of the shirt has been chosen from among the standards on offer, collars and sleeves are selected to match your own size.

What then remains is the choice of material. Offering a silken look, the Sea Islands – very long-fibered cotton – is the finest and most becoming. The sobriety of the poplin suits a classic shirt, while the weight lends the garment a most relaxed style.

Trench coats: not to be ditched

These "coats from the trenches" were designed by English soldiers posted to the front at Verdun. Much popularized ever since, to the point of assimilation into everyday language, the paternity of the trench coat lies at the core of a dispute between Aquascutum and Burberry, it being claimed by both. However that may be, production by both companies (see p. 98) is of equally excellent quality: both distribute this cream-colored overcoat-cum-city dweller garment, usually lined with tartan. But it is at Burberry's where you can have your initials embroidered on the inside of the coat, an important detail if your friends are as snobbish as you are. Remember to have it regularly waterproofed by a specialist.

Tweed for all seasons

Where would British elegance be without its legendary tweed? The most famous and the best of all these Anglo-Saxon fabrics is certainly the Harris tweed, used primarily for jackets. It comes exclusively from the island of the same name in the north of Scotland. Of artisan craftsmanship, it is made up of pure new wool from Scottish or Irish sheep.

It is available in three different weights: standard (perfect for fall and winter coats), light (reserved for summer clothes) and bantam (for the hottest climates), in case you wish to undertake a cruise along the Nile, or you want to look like an officer in the Indian army.

Hats: from bowlers to panamas

Designed in 1850 by farmer William Bowler to protect his gamekeepers' heads from the branches, it was in London that the famous bowler hat (derby hat) had its hour of glory. No longer popular today, it was at one time a huge success among the employees of the City. But it was evidently Charlie Chaplin who immortalized it. If you don't want to look like Charlie Chaplin, nor like John Steed, you can always find a cap more suited to your taste, or a perennially fashionable panama hat, at Lock's (see below).

A SMALL ITINERARY OF MASCULINE FASHION

Jermyn Street is to be particularly recommended for its shirts. It crosses St. James's Street, where you will find two of the most fashionable addresses, Lobb and Lock. Crossing Piccadilly, you will soon come to Savile Row, home to the greatest tailors. Nearby Regent Street allows you to visit the department stores of Aquascutum and Austin Reed, where the art-deco hairdressers and barbers salon is a classic.

Jelly, pudding
and mint sauce

The English eat more and more like their counterparts in continental Europe, with food particularly heavily influenced by French, Italian and Asian cuisine. This in turn affects the food available in the stores and supermarkets with much of the produce originating outside the UK. As far as British gastronomy is concerned, those particularities which sometimes alarmed the visitor are also being toned down as a result of the influence of world cuisine. Rich tastes, ripe cheeses, garlic and chili all appear with increasing frequency in the meals now served up.

Fast food

Fast food has developed considerably over the past 20 years or so. Apart from the ubiquitous McDonalds and its competitors, London boasts many hundreds of fast food outlets, some of which, such as Angus Steak House specializing in unimaginative grills, are homegrown. Unless you have children with you, or need a meal in a hurry, avoid them! More typically British, and often better value, are the so-called "greasy spoon" cafés These serve "fry-ups" — fried eggs, bacon, sausages, chips, etc. — together with large mugs of tea or coffee and buttered toast.

ish 'n' Chips

he famous "fish 'n' chips" is
very British way of providing
heap fast food. This is a fried
d or haddock fillet sprinkled
ith vinegar and served with
rge chips. To respect the
onventions, you have it
rapped in paper and eat it with
our fingers. Absolutely delicious
ut loaded with calories.

airy products

he English consume 118
ters (250 pints) of milk per
erson per year, and there are
o fewer than a hundred

ifferent varieties of cheese in
reat Britain. The habit of
ating cheese after dessert,
ccompanied by a glass of
ort, has almost disappeared,
ut the English have
ediscovered their local cheeses
n recent years, sometimes
avored with parsley, sage or
ther herbs, which haven't
een popular for a long time.

Mad cows and Englishmen

ou need not worry about
atching mad cow disease from
ating British beef. Today it is
trictly controlled, even Scotch

Angus which is one of the best.
If you suffer from paranoia
stick to lamb or chicken.

World cuisine

London is home to restaurants
representing cuisines from
almost every corner of the
world and reflecting the
multicultural population. The
most common types of ethnic
food are Indian, Italian, Thai
and Chinese, but in London
you can find pretty much
anything you want.

Vegetarian cuisine

The latest
surveys report
that around seven
percent of the UK
population
considers itself to
be vegetarian –
and this percentage
may be higher in the
capital. Vegetarian restaurants
are becoming increasingly
sophisticated and popular.
Indian cuisine is traditionally
vegetarian and the many local
Indian restaurants have
a wide selection of vegetable-
based dishes.

SWEET TOOTH – A TASTE FOR CANDY

The English have a sweet tooth and consume a
substantial amount of sugar in all its forms.
Traditional steamed desserts – with eccentric names
such as "spotted dick" (with raisins) and "jam roly-
poly" – are talked about with nostalgia but are not as
popular as they once were in these more health-
conscious times. However, some, such as "sticky
toffee pudding," are making a comeback. Christmas
pudding, a very rich steamed fruit pudding, is served
only at Christmas dinner with cream or brandy butter.
By contrast, other "puddings" (a generic term meaning
dessert) are mostly pies and tarts served with custard,
and ice cream and "jelly" (jello) for the children.
The English are above all partial to candy and eat more
of it than any other nation in the world.
You'll be surprised at
the amount of shelf
space allocated at the
newsagent to chocolate,
fruit candy and chewing
gum of all types. Watch
your cavities if you try
the blocks of toffee.
And restaurants routinely
bring a mint chocolate to
be eaten with a coffee.

This is an official London Sightseein

London,
the cultural capital

It is impossible to complete a tour of London's culture in a weekend, or in two pages! The city brings together the best in world theater, an excellent dance and classical music scene and has some of the most beautiful and original museums. Here we offer you a foretaste, which will whet your appetite for further visits in the future.

The world capital of free spirits

A place of sanctuary and of inspiration, many famous writers and artists have found in London a haven of peace. Freud, fleeing Nazi Germany in 1938, took up residence here. It is possible today to visit his home and consulting rooms (20 Maresfield Gdns, ☎ 0207 435 20 02, Mon.-Wed. 12-5pm). Other great historical figures in search of freedom

have chosen London. General de Gaulle established the headquarters of the Free French from whence he issued the Appeal of June 18. Claude Monet took refuge here during the war of 1870; *Westminster Bridge* is testimony to his sojourn. At the beginning of the 20th century, the painter André Derain also took inspiration from the Thames and applied Fauvist colors to his *London*

Bridge. Two illustrious German composers adopted London: George Frederick Handel went so far as to adop British nationality in 1726, while in 1877 Richard Wagne directed the orchestra of the Royal Albert Hall. It was also in London that Karl Marx wrote *Das Kapital*. American writers such as Mark Twain

Karl Marx at work in Londo

nd Henry James pursued
eir work on the banks of
e Thames. Whether for
rief visits or permanent
sidences, London's cultural
adiance has also attracted
udents such as Gandhi,
ho left India in order to
ndertake his law studies in
e metropolis. Also of Indian
rigin, the British novelist
alman Rushdie found in
ondon conditions conducive
success.

Contemporary art

ach year, the Tate (Millbank,
☎ 0207 887 80 00, every day
0am-5.30pm) awards the
urner prize to the best among
ontemporary British artists.

Modern furniture
t the Tate Gallery.

stablished artists, such as the
isual artists Gilbert and
George, are exhibited at the
nthony d'Offay gallery
9, 21, 23 and 24 Dering St;
Mon.-Fri. 10am-5.30pm, Sat.
-5.30pm). The Chisenhale
Gallery, by contrast, is more
nterested in the rising stars
f English art including
isa Milroy or the Wilson
isters (64 Chisenhale Rd,
☎ 0208 981 45 18, Wed.-Sat.
-6pm). Finally, for lovers of
hotography this address is

essential: the Photographer's
Gallery (5-8 Great Newport St,
☎ 0207 831 17 72, every day
11am-6pm).

Theater

With about a hundred theaters,
London remains faithful to the
tradition that has William
Shakespeare as its figurehead.
The Royal National Theatre
(South Bank, ☎ 0207 628 33
51) and the Royal Shakespeare
Company (Barbican Centre
☎ 0207 382 72 72) devote
themselves to classical
repertory. The theaters along
Shaftesbury Avenue are where
you go to see the musicals,
which always attract such

large crowds. More intimate
and avant-garde productions
are to be found in smaller
theaters in the suburbs.
Here they are known as
"fringe" theaters.

Music

Some of the London orchestras
also contribute to the global
renown of the capital: The
famous Royal Albert Hall plays
host to the no less famous
Royal Philharmonic
Orchestra, directed by Daniele
Gatti. John Eliot Gardiner's
orchestra, the Orchestra of the
Age of Enlightenment, has a
particular reputation for
playing Baroque music.

ORIGINAL MUSEUMS

The famous wax statues
can be seen at **Madame
Tussaud's** (Marylebone
Rd, ☎ 0870 400 30 00,
www.madametussaud.com,
every day. 9am-5.30pm). This
has had some competition
ever since **Rock Circus**
(London Pavilion, 1 Piccadilly
Circus, ☎ 0207 734 72 03)
began presenting its doubles
of famous pop stars. If you
have children, visit **London
Transport Museum.** (Covent
Garden ☎ 0207 379 63 44).

United colors
of London

Beneath the gray of a London sky, the city presents a swarm of colors and smells which bear witness to its colonial heritage and the connections it still maintains with distant countries now joined together, since gaining their independence, within the Commonwealth. It is the coexistence of communities of such varied origins which gives London its cosmopolitan character, supported by a long tradition of freedom and openness. It is for these reasons that discovering London means becoming acquainted with other cultures and going on a trip around the world.

The colors of India

London is home to the largest Indian community in Europe: 525,000 Indians, Pakistanis and Bengalis live in the capital today.
A visit to Southall, home to the Sikh community, will immerse you in oriental exoticism: displays by fabric merchants and jewelers (but beware, the quality of the gold can be as low as

nine carats). The Indian restaurants are the other jewel of this neighborhood: a must.

Black music

Among London's black community of 450,000 people, it is the Jamaicans who are most numerous. The liveliness of Brixton market will give you a typical insight (see p. 122).

you are drawn to places
ore off the beaten track,
me of the most hip black
ibs are to be found in
ilston, near Ridley Road,
. And, of course, the Notting
ll Carnival, London's big
ro-Caribbean festival, is
orth the trip in itself.
iring the last weekend in
igust, 500,000 people
tend a completely manic
ocession, dancing to the
inds of soul and reggae.

hinatown

he district of Soho around
errard Street (see p. 53)
as been the heart of the
iinese community for
ore than 30 years. A large
imber of its 55,000
embers originate from
ong Kong. If you are
rtunate enough to be in
ondon toward the end of
inuary, you can watch the
stivities surrounding the
iinese New Year, where
ains of people disguised as
ragons parade through the
reets of the area to ward
ff evil spirits.

mirs and mosques

he Muslim community is
ot only larger than the other
iinorities (800,000 Muslims
ve on British soil), it is also
ie most varied. While the
mirs of the Gulf display a
rand style within the capital,
irge numbers of immigrants
ve very modestly. Islamic
atherings can be seen
egularly at Trafalgar
quare. In Whitechapel
coad, the East London
Mosque, recently opened
ianks to Arab funding, is a
appy mixture of modern
esign and traditional
rchitecture.

St Patrick's Day

Westminster Cathedral
(Morpeth Terrace) and St.
Patrick's Church (Soho Sq.)
are the two rallying points
for the Irish community
(250,000 members). Each
year on St Patrick's Day —
the patron saint of Ireland —
they take over both the
churches and the pubs, and
the beer flows like water.

European melting pot

On July 16 the Italian
community gathers to
organize a huge procession
in honor of the Virgin Mary.

It takes place at St. Peter's
Church in Clerkenwell,
and brings together many of
the 75,000 Italians living
in London. The Jewish
community is concentrated
around Golders Green and
Ilford. At the beginning of
World War Two the Polish
also took refuge in the city;
today they number 50,000.
Finally, some 40,000 French
people have established
themselves in the capital of
"perfidious Albion," living
primarily in Kensington,
where you can find French
grocery stores, bakers and
bookstores.

THE COMMONWEALTH INSTITUTE

Located in a very chic residential district, the
Commonwealth Institute is a strange construction
built in the shape of a tent, and traces the history and
culture of the 50 countries born of the British Empire
now joined together since their independence within
the Commonwealth. Temporary exhibitions and
concerts are regularly organized.
**Kensington High St, High Street Kensington Tube
☎ 0207 603 45 35, Mon.-Sat. 10am-5pm.**

Tableware
and china

There was a resurgence during the 18th century of the British tradition of manufacturing fine china, and this vast production rapidly became a national specialty. You will often find entire services at very reasonable prices. If you want to have the British touch, look especially for little cake plates or trays for a cake assortment, or even a cake-stand: multi-level platters which are used to serve cakes at teatime.

Tableware

Western tableware is heir to medieval glazed pottery. The raw clay is molded or turned before being dried out in an oven and then submersed in a bath of enamel. Once this has dried, the item is painted, then baked fiercely for at least 30 hours in order to fix the colors. Today one may uncover the most beautiful pieces of antique tableware in the specialist shops but modern tableware, often with reproductions of floral motifs or of English pastoral scenes in red or pastel blue, is much cheaper and of good quality. It is easy to clean and dishwasher-safe.

Bone china

It is to its base material – kaolin – that bone china owes its whiteness and its translucid appearance.

eated in China, it has
en of interest to European
anufacturers since the
th century. The English
mediately introduced
rtain variations, such as
e addition of bone cinders
to the clay. This process,
vented in 1800, has given
name to fine porcelain.
his time the items are baked
ice: The first time to bake
e enamel (a vitreous
ating which gives a shiny
pearance) for about
hours, the second time,
ther gently or at fierce
eat, finally sets the colors
d patterns.

Spode

he great name in English
orcelain, the Spode brand
as existed since 1770.
was in fact its creator
osiah Spode who developed
he art of manufacturing
one china in 1800. Today it
emains appreciated for its
wo superior classic designs:
tafford Flowers, created at
he beginning of the 19th
entury, easily recognizable
y its inspired botanical
esigns, (£160 for a 27cm/
1in plate), and the Blue
talian, with blue and white
astoral decoration (£9 for a
7cm/11in plate).

Royal Worcester

This was one of the principal
brands of English bone china
in the 18th century. Since
that era, it has been able to
simultaneously develop its
production of tableware while
improving its durability.
Today the same qualities are
to be found among its range
of tableware which is not
only microwave- but also
oven- and freezer-safe.
Royal Doulton also
produces durable quality
tableware.

Wedgwood, the last word in fine bone china

Created in 1750, Wedgwood
designs were initially
modeled on precious stones.
Between 1764 and 1774, its
creator Josiah Wedgwood

concentrated on the
manufacture of creamware, a
white porcelain designed to
compete with Sèvres and
Meissen. Later, the discovery
of black biscuit (basalt)
permitted the development
of an extraordinary
monochrome design which
was followed during the 19th
century by blue and white
biscuit. Still manufactured
today, its original designs
have been expanded to
hundreds of different pieces
of tableware, all of which are
of a refined appearance.

On the underside of the tableware, you will find the
potter's trademark, either in letters or as a monogram.
The more prestigious the trademark is, the more
expensive the item. The more rare or exceptional
pieces will also carry the artist's signature or the seal
of the studio where the piece was decorated.
All these elements are important because, if you
ever need to sell it, they will be taken into
consideration by your purchaser.

Large checks
and little flowers

Couturiers will not regret relocating to London, since fabrics for both furnishings and clothing are plentiful, reasonably priced and often of an inimitable style. Woolens are not always of better value than elsewhere, but the quality and spectrum of choice firmly place them on the list of purchases you can make with your eyes closed.

Tartans: from Highland clans to rugby matches

The genuine tartan is a worsted serge fabric; it has a right and a wrong way round. Originally (prior to the 12th century), the wearing of a tartan had a social significance: It enabled members of the same clan to be identified by their patterns. It is of this material that kilts are made today, although they are only worn on special occasions (rugby matches or official ceremonies).

There are many hundreds of different designs. The clans of Campbell, Leslie or MacArthur are distinguished by a dominant green, while those of Hay, Frazer, MacFie or Wallace are marked by a dominant red. The Chattan clan distinguishes itself in a more fanciful manner. In an interior setting, a tartan is ideal for creating an atmosphere of rustic luxury: for curtains in soft silk, heavy wool for re-covering an old sofa, or even a carpet for a corridor or a stairwell.

Chintz in all its glory

Chintz is a generic term denoting fabrics printed with a floral pattern. First imported from India during the 16th and 17th centuries, it has been copied and

Double-knitted, lambswool is very hardwearing and is safe to machine-wash. Marks & Spencer's lambswool, for example, is of excellent quality, especially for menswear; some of their mottled colors are truly splendid.

Not tarred with the same brush

Sweaters from the Isle of Arran are single-knit woolens, either pure or unbleached, thick-ribbed or cable-knit, sometimes incorrectly called "Irish pullovers." Ideally, such items are best handknitted. Originally they were made by fishermen's wives from this Scottish island located in the Clyde estuary, west of Glasgow. In order to identify the corpses of their husbands if they happened to drown at sea, the women of Arran all knitted different designs. It is for this reason that in Britain these sweaters are called fisherman's sweaters.

manufactured in Great Britain since 1680. Originally a furnishings fabric, it has equally been adapted as a wallpaper by Laura Ashley and Colefax and Fowler. There is also the Liberty brand, an excellent chintz ready to make into all kinds of clothing.

Gentle as a lamb

Both Shetland and lambswool can be used to knit excellent pullovers, the type you always love to wear and which get increasingly comfortable as time passes. Shetland is a very warm and durable wool, covered in a soft down, the product of sheep from the islands of the same name in the north of Scotland. By tradition, pullovers made of this wool never go out of fashion: crew neck or V-neck and in classic colors, although fashionable shades are seen more and more often.

Preferably choose a very dense quality wool which will last a long time. Lambswool is softer and finer than Shetland.

COLEFAX AND FOWLER

39 Brook St,
☎ 0207 493 22 31
Bond Street Tube
Mon.-Fri. 9.30am-5.30pm.
The collection of chintz fabric sold by this establishment is one of the most beautiful in all London. Specialty of the house is the notable reproductions of 19th-century designs, and each year new motifs are added to the collection to enlarge an already impressive catalog. The atmosphere of the store is that of an English country house, where the chintz billows at the windows, adorns the tables and adds frills to the cushions.

The art of
lifting the little finger

When traveling to London, it's now or never to sample the British national beverage. Numerous teahouses with elegant subdued ambiences will open their arms to you, and several stores are devoted exclusively to this infusion. You will find the most extensive range in the world, not just of tea but also of the china to accompany it: fanciful or sophisticated teapots, entire tea sets, covered teapots, etc. You will inevitably discover the accessories to match your own interior and lifestyle, and the brand of tea to match your temperament.

What is tea?

Tea comes from the leaf of the tea plant, a bush which grows on the sides of a hill. If the leaves aren't treated, the tea will be green; but if they are allowed to ferment, they produce a black tea. Scented tea leaves are dried over a wood fire. The quality varies according to its place of origin — essentially India, China or Sri Lanka — and to the type of teapot used.

Natural essences, from the traditional bergamot to the more unusual such as banana or coconut, are also sometimes added.

How do the English drink it?

Pouring the milk before the tea allows the leaves to remain at the bottom of the cup. By contrast, lemon is best added afterward.

Coarsely crushed candied sugar is the best type to add to tea. To help it dissolve, add it before the lemon. You may be surprised to learn that more and more tea and coffeehouses serve tea bags, something which for a long while was considered heresy, but they are so much more practical!

Which tea to drink?

If you drink tea in the morning, it is better to select a scented tea such as Lapsang Souchong, which is strongly perfumed. English Breakfast tea is very popular and usually of excellent quality even if bought from non-specialists such as Marks & Spencer. In the afternoon, preferably choose Afternoon Tea or try a scented mixture.

Fans of the Royal family prefer the Flowery Orange Keemun Pekoe (from China), which was drunk at Buckingham Palace on the Queen's anniversary. Earl Grey tea, flavored with bergamot, goes well with fish, whereas Darjeeling goes better with poultry or spicy dishes.

Madhatter's tea party

In London you will find teapots of all kinds, from the most classical to the most eccentric, from the shape of a double-decker bus to that of an British letterbox (mailbox). These are without doubt the finest and most ornate porcelain with the most British look. They go well with both traditional and scented teas. If you prefer a full-bodied tea, then select a teapot made of pewter or, better still, of silver: the finest of the fine. For scented teas, a teapot made of glass is to be preferred, since the odors will not linger. To prevent your teapot from becoming musty when not in use, leave it open with a lump of sugar in the bottom.

For eating and drinking

Many English specialties seem to have been conceived for no other purpose than to accompany tea: scones, small heavy cakes made with raisins; crumpets, a kind of aerated crepe; and the famous English muffins. Scones can be eaten either dry or buttered, although the true English prefer them with fresh cream and strawberry jam. The romantic ideal "high tea" is always accompanied by cucumber or watercress sandwiches which go remarkably well with tea.

PRESERVING TEA

Be sure to keep tea separate from any strongly scented products that might affect its flavor. Tea is delicate and it requires protecting from air, light, humidity and heat. It should ideally be kept in a hermetically sealed metal container. Classic teas will keep for up to two years and scented teas for 12 months.

The British
way of life

Even though London follows the same pace of life as other European capitals, you often feel you are in a veritable haven of peace. Take a stroll and discover London through its streets, a perfect example of the celebrated British way of life. At the end of the day and of the week, it is a very different London that you meet, and very different British people, too.

After work...

London is too often summed up by the frantic life of the City and its "white collar" workers. Its vitality is certainly amazing considering that this capital is one of the epicenters of world trade. But in England, work remains above all a way of making a living in order to do what you want after the hours spent at the office. That is why Londoners often wake up at the crack of dawn. They begin early in order to finish early and to enjoy the rest of the day. Moreover, Sunday has remained a very special

day in which idleness reigns supreme.

... taking comfort

The pub is one of the great institutions of London life. Every street has its own pub and every pub has its own clientele. On leaving the office it is not uncommon for colleagues to discuss things over a pint of beer. As a national drink, beer flows freely always in a noisy and convivial din. Most pubs are open between 11am and 11pm. In England, the

...ajority of pleasant evenings ...gin in a pub, sitting at an ...l wooden bar, beer in hand. ...u are bound to make ...ends here. For a guaranteed ...mosphere, be sure not to ...ss a screened soccer match, ...unforgettable moment!

...sound mind in a ...ealthy body

...gland has been the ...untry of origin for ...merous sporting activities. ...oquet, cricket and polo can ...l trace their roots to the ...story of this country. And if ...e saying is true that a ...und mind resides in a ...und body then the British ...rtainly make good use of it. ...st watch the number of ...ggers along the streets and ...the parks. The capital also ...sts more than a dozen ...ofessional soccer teams, ...ch neighborhood staunchly ...oud of its own. Tennis is ...ot forgotten, however, and is ...presented most significantly

by the Wimbledon tournament. The less adventurous can always devote themselves to a game of darts.

Green and pleasant

London is without doubt one of the leafiest capitals in Europe, with approximately 30 percent of its surface area composed of green spaces. Fresh air is provided by a multitude of parks and gardens. A place to relax par excellence, these leafy corners are put to good use by all. At noon, businessmen come

here to eat their packed lunch. In summer, everyone takes the opportunity to unbutton their shirt and lounge in the sun. A sight not to be missed! If you like large open spaces, you have almost a dozen parks to choose from. The most famous are Regent's Park (with its zoo and its rose garden), Hyde Park (the largest) and St James's Park (near Buckingham Palace), full of little squirrels.

Place your bets

Throughout Great Britain gambling is legal and almost every high street has a branch of a "betting shop," offering odds in the window for the latest horserace or soccer tournament. In London, such practices have become a real obsession. Some inveterate gamblers will not hesitate to risk several pounds on what color hat the Queen will wear next, or on the next front cover of the *Sun*, the benchmark daily tabloid newspaper. For smaller spenders, bingo is one of the more playful activities. Hundreds of devotees gather together every weekend in special clubs dedicated to this lottery-style game.

HAVING A HEART

In London, charities are well developed and it is a rare Englishman who is not a member of an association, be it charitable, sporting or otherwise. In fact there is a multitude of organizations regularly attempting to raise funds, whether from competitions, shows, sale items or clothing. Moreover, in pursuit of this generous activity, some organizations have opened stores which devote a proportion of their turnover to charitable undertakings.

Practicalities

Getting around

London is much larger than many other European cities and its principal sights are often equally as far apart from each other. You could hardly hope to see the whole city in a single day!

In order to get around, you can use the subway, buses and taxis, as well as commuter trains for traveling toward the outskirts – known as Greater London. If public transport-

FINDING YOUR WAY AROUND

You will find details of the nearest subway (Tube) station after the address in the What to See section, as well as maps for each of the suggested walks.

ation seems expensive, this is because it in fact receives very little subsidy either from the state or from the city itself. For a weekend vacation, the best idea would be to purchase a 3 Day Travelcard. This allows you to travel as often as you wish on the subway and on all buses in the capital, except night buses (after midnight). It costs £15 for zones 1 and 2, which you will be unlikely to leave considering the location of most attractions. Along the same lines there is also the One Day Travelcard (costing £4.70 for zones 1 and 2), which is valid from 9.30am onward. All such cards can be purchased at Heathrow airport (zone 6) at a slightly higher cost (£6 for a One Day Travelcard), which can be offset against your trip into London.

The Tube (subway)

The London subway (or "Tube") has always been a nightmare for overseas visitors, but it is now much improved. It is nowadays the quickest way to get around London. The trains run from 5.30am to midnight, except on Christmas Day. Directions are clearly marked but if you encounter any difficulty do not hesitate to ask a member of staff – they are very helpful. The waiting time and the destination of each train are clearly indicated on each platform. Don't forget to keep hold of your ticket, you will need it to get out of the station. At the end of your journey, it is possible that someone at the exit could ask for your travel card: These cards are not individualized and this custom is widespread.

wever, the practice is illegal
d the touts are criminals.
u shouldn't be tempted to
nd over your card.

uses

ses are slower than the
bway but offer a more
inquil way to visit the city,
rticularly if you sit on the
pper story of a double-decker,
e famous London bus.
you don't already have a
cket, you can buy one from
e driver but make sure you
ve change. Some bus
utes are especially useful
r getting to districts poorly
rved by the Tube. Buses are
so a good way of getting
ound at night, between
pm and 6am. The bus
imbers at that time are
efixed with a capital N.
nong the most useful bus
utes, the number 15 will
ing you from the British
useum to South Kensington
a Piccadilly Circus, the 168
ll take you from Oxford
reet or from Piccadilly
rcus to St. Paul's, and the
"A leaves Charing Cross for
estminster. You need to
gnal to the driver in order to
et the bus to stop.

low to use
he telephone

o telephone London from
verseas, dial 0044 followed
y the number required but
nitting the 0. To make a call
om within London, the 0
ust precede the number
quired. There are two area
odes: (0) 207 and (0) 208,
e latter being reserved for
uter London. To make a call
o North America from within
ie UK, dial 001 and then the
rea code and number

required. British telephone
booths are of two types: the
old-style BT (British Telecom)
traditional red boxes, and new
hooded booths. Some only
accept credit cards or
telephone cards, but these are
often located next to booths
that accept 20p or 50p coins.
Telephone cards can be

purchased at post offices
and at newsagents. They
exist in denominations of
£2, £4 and £10. There are
now also international cards
at preferential rates. A
conversation of several
minutes will cost 20p in
London. Charges are lower
after 6pm during the week,

TAXIS

There are two types of taxi in London: black cabs
(licensed) and minicabs. You can easily recognize
regular taxis by their shape, even if they have traded
their traditional black attire for a more fanciful color,
or even for advertising.

If available for hire, the yellow sign on the roof will be
lit, and will say "For Hire" at the rear. There is a
minimum fee plus an additional charge per minute.
Luggage, extra passengers and hire at nighttime will
attract supplementary charges.

Minicabs are special vehicles providing services
directly, particularly at night when the black cabs are
less common. Be careful and agree the fare before
getting into the vehicle. If you have any concerns,
you can always call a taxi company, such as Lady
Cabs (for women traveling alone, ☎ 0207 254 3501).
For general inquiries ☎ 0207 286 0286. If you have
left something in a taxi cab, call lost and found
☎ 0207 486 2496 Mon.-Fri. 9am-4pm.

but there again the rate on offer will be quite unfavorabl If you have an American Express card, go directly to one of their branches (to find these, go to www.americanexpress.com), at least you will not have to pay a commission charge.

A useful address if you need t change currency in an emergency is:
Cheque Point,
548 Oxford St
Marble Arch Tube
☎ 0207 723 10 05.
Open 24 hours.

If you withdraw cash using a debit card, which is increasingly beneficial, try to do this in one go because a fixed commission will be charged by your bank for each withdrawal made.

and throughout the weekend. Most cafés and pubs no longer have coin-operated public phones due to the fact that almost all customers have their own cell phones. Calls from a hotel are usually subject to surcharges.

Mail

To mail something outside Great Britain, purchase stamps at post offices or at newsagents displaying the sign "Stamps sold here." There is one price for mail within the EU and tiered rates outside the EU. The large red mailboxes are easily recognized, they carry the Royal Mail logo and often have a slot especially for overseas mail.

Banks and bureaus de change

Banks are open Monday to Friday from 9.30am to 4.00pm, and some of them also Saturday morning until noon. To change currency on Saturday afternoons, you will need to go to one of the many bureaus de change (Thomas Cook or Cheque Point) located throughout the tourist districts. Be aware, though, that these branches will most likely offer an unfavorable rate of exchange and that they will charge a commission. Avoid changing money at the hotel, this is most disadvantageous. Department stores often have their own bureaus de change,

Tourist information centers

British Travel Centr
1 Regent Street
Piccadilly Circus Tube
Mon.-Fri. 9am-6.30pm,
Sat.-Sun. 10am-4pm.

LONDON BY NIGHT

As in all capital cities, many tours of London are on offer to tourists in the evening. If you prefer to travel by bus, then it's the following:
☎ 0207 233 70 30
or the river bus
☎ 0207 839 35 72.

re you will find information
ochures (sights and maps)
well as a bookstore, a
uvenir shop and a bureau
change. The staff can
sily help and advise you
ere to find accommodations,
make a reservation for
how or a place for a
htseeing tour, or to indicate
ich train will take you to
eenwich.

ondon Tourist
oard

e branches of the London
urist Board are located close
tourist attractions. There
u can obtain free street
aps and information on
aces to visit, trips on the
ver Thames, organized
cursions, shows and cultural
ents. They can also help you
d a hotel. Or you can also
ephone on ☎ 0870 588
11, for a prerecording
the most important
formation.

OPENING HOURS FOR THE PRINCIPAL SIGHTS

The museums and monuments are in general open
between 10am and 5pm Monday through Saturday
(there is little difference between summer and winter).
Some, such as the British Museum, are open between
noon and 6pm on Sundays. There are no rest days
during the week, although all are closed December 24
to 26, January 1 and Good Friday.

The White Card is a voucher valid for either three or
seven days which gives entry to the 13 largest
museums of the city, but this is of relatively little
benefit since many institutions are free. When there
is a charge, museums and monuments always offer a
reduction for children and students. Even if entry is
free, there is nothing to stop you making a small
donation to the work of the museum.

Heathrow Airport
Terminals 1, 2 and 3
Every day 8.30am-6pm.

Liverpool Street Station
Liverpool St. Tube
Mon.-Sat. 8.15am-6pm,
Sun. 8.30am-6.45pm.

Selfridges
Basement Arcade,
Selfridges. Mon.-Fri.
9.30am-7pm, Sat. until
6.30am.

Victoria Station Forecourt
Victoria Station, 8am-7pm.
Victoria Station Forecourt
Has a good bookstore and
souvenir shop.

Waterloo International Terminal
Arrival Hall, Waterloo Tube.
8am-7pm.
Very handy if you arrive by
Eurostar.

What to see in London
and sights not to miss

To make your discovery of the city easier, we have prepared 14 walks around London, each illustrated with its own map. If you only have limited time at your disposal, here is a selection of 12 essential things to see. They are all covered elsewhere in the guide and you will also find them in more detail at the end of the What to See chapter.

Buckingham Palace

Come and admire the palace of the Royal family, especially at 11.30am, the time of the famous Changing of the Guard.

See walk no. 1 p. 38 and Don't Miss p. 74

Westminster Abbey

It is in this magnificent building that most English monarchs have been both crowned and buried.

See walk no. 1 p. 38 and Don't Miss p. 75

Westminster Palace

When you visit this huge edifice don't miss the opportunity to stop at the famous Big Ben clock and set your watch.

See walk no. 1 p. 39 and Don't Miss p. 76

National Gallery

The Grand Masters of the 13th to the 20th centuries on display here make for one of the most beautiful museums in the world. Absolutely a must-see.

See walk no. 6 p. 52 and Don't Miss p. 77

Trafalgar Square

Do not miss this London square. A tourist attraction by day and a sea of people on festive evenings.

See walk no. 6 p. 52 and Don't Miss p. 78

Kensington Palace

After visiting this vast palace, Kensington Gardens, effectively an extension of Hyde Park, are an ideal place for a stroll.

See walk no. 11 p. 67 and Don't Miss p. 83

British Museum

A true British institution, this museum – more popular than the Louvre – covers the history of mankind from its origins to the present day.

See walk no. 10 p. 64 and Don't Miss p. 79

Saint Paul's Cathedral

Notable for its spectacular Whispering Gallery and the external gallery which gives a magnificent view over London.

See walk no. 12 p. 68 and Don't Miss p. 81

Tate Britain

With a collection mainly of work by modern artists, this museum is worth seeing as a complement to the National Gallery.

See walk no. 13 p. 70 and Don't Miss p. 84

Victoria and Albert Museum

The 145 rooms in this museum dedicated to both fine and applied art contain one of the richest collections of its kind.

See walk no. 4 p. 48 and Don't Miss p. 82

Tower of London

Guarding London from the 11th century, the Tower is a symbol of the city's past.

See walk no. 12 p. 68 and Don't Miss p. 80

Tate Modern

A place worth seeing for the development of this industrial site turned museum and for the works of art from the 19th century to the present day which are on display here.

See walk no. 13 p. 70 and Don't Miss p. 85

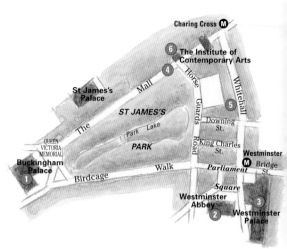

Charing Cross Ⓜ

6 The Institute of
Contemporary Arts

4

St James's
Palace

The Mall

Horse Guards

Whitehall

ST JAMES'S

5

The

Park Lake

Downing
St.

QUEEN
VICTORIA
MEMORIAL

PARK

King Charles
St.

Buckingham
Palace

1

Road

Westminster

Ⓜ

Bridge

Birdcage   Walk   Parliament St.

Square

Westminster
Abbey

2

3

Westminster
Palace

Westminster
and Royal London

In a single walk you will discover one of the
most beautiful abbeys in the world, the centers
of power of English political life and two royal
palaces. As would be expected, you will meet
more Japanese and French people here than
Londoners, and shops are also a rarity. To
make things easier for yourself, it's better to
begin your visit to this area at Westminster,
with its palace and its abbey, when the
majority of tourists are in front of Buckingham
Palace for the Changing of the Guard. Then you
will meet the crowds coming the other way.

❶ Buckingham Palace★★★

The Mall
☎ 0207 321 22 33
Aug-Sep. Every day 9.30am-
4.15pm; guided tours every
15 minutes. Changing of the
Guard every day at 11.30am,
every other day in winter.
Entry fee

The famous residence of the
Queen of England such as you

see it today dates from the
beginning of the 19th century
(except the façade, which dates
from 1913). It was the architect
John Nash who transformed the
original manor house (of
1705) into a huge palace,
conceived from the beginning
as simply a pied-à-terre for
King George IV. In order to

finance the reconstruction of
the palace of the Windsors,
recently damaged by fire, some
rooms are open to the public
during the summer, as long as
the monarch is on vacation.

❷ Westminster Abbey★★★

Broad Sanctuary
☎ 0207 222 51 52
Mon.-Fri. 9.15am-4.45pm

of Commons and the House of Lords. This is the heart of English political life: Three thousand people work here in a thousand offices and two miles of corridors. It is above all for its clock, familiarly called Big Ben (after Benjamin Hall, who directed the work of installing it) that the palace is best known. It is possible to go inside the clock tower to observe the mechanism, if you have the courage to climb! The famous chimes of Big Ben

can be heard within a radius of two miles around Westminster.

❹ The Mall★★

This was already a fashionable place in 1660, even though it was little more than a simple alley lined with trees. It wasn't until 1911 that this broad avenue was constructed by the

same architect who built the Admiralty Arch in homage to Queen Victoria. The mall runs along St James's Park, the oldest of London's parks and one of the most pleasant. Dairymen pastured their cows here in the 19th century. Today you can see pelicans here.

❺ Whitehall★★★

Walking down Whitehall toward Trafalgar Square, you will come across Downing Street. For reasons of security, you are not allowed to enter this road, but you can see on your left one of the façades of the Foreign Office. On your right, No. 10 contains the offices of the Prime Minister in a building which dates from 1684; the Cabinet Office and the Scottish Office are there also.

st admission at 3.45pm), at. 9.15am-2.45pm (last dmission at 1.45pm); osed Sundays except for rvices

rst and foremost, it will be the bey exterior with its flying ttresses which will hold your tention. Then, in the interior, ose most short of time will ant to see as a matter of riority the Nave — especially if ey are fond of stained-glass ndows — and Henry VII's hapel with its extraordinary ults. If you go to the Abbey useum, which gathers gether the honored dead, be re to see the statue of Henry II and you will notice some air beneath his ears. pparently they were caught in e mold when his mortuary ask was being made.

❸ Westminster Palace★★★

Parliament Square
☎ 0207 219 30 00
House of Commons:
Mon.-Thu. 2.30-10pm,
Wed. from 9.30am,
Fri. 9.30am-3pm. Telephone n advance to make a reservation for a guided our

A neo-Gothic edifice built in the 19th century, Westminster Palace contains both the House

❻ THE INSTITUTE OF CONTEMPORARY ARTS

(Carlton House Terrace)
The Mall
☎ 0207 930 36 47
Every day 12-7.30pm.
Sponsored by Toshiba, the Institute of Contemporary Arts has collections of both English and international avant-garde art. Hurry to the bookstore to purchase *Frieze*, one of the best art magazines, and stop a while at the very comfortable bar.

2

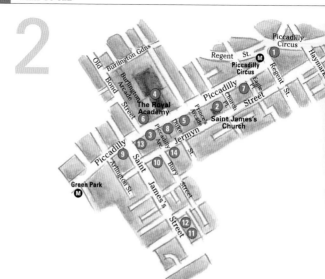

Between Piccadilly Circus and Green Park

Piccadilly could easily be to London what the Champs-Elysées are to Paris: an elegant commercial thoroughfare uniquely symbolizing the city. Along its length are to be found some of the most compelling locations for a London vacation, from Wedgwood to Fortnum and Mason's. Less gridlocked than Oxford Street, shopping is more relaxed here (and more expensive!). Don't miss Jermyn Street either, with its menswear stores, or St James's Street with its purveyors to the Crown.

❶ Piccadilly Circus★★

This is without doubt one of the most famous places in London. Dominating it, the statue of Eros drawing a bow seems to be mischievously taking aim at passers-by, or at the eccentrics for whom the fountain is a rallying point. Piccadilly Circus has to be seen by night, when the neon signs are lit up in all their colors. Not to be missed is Tower Records, a gigantic

music store open until midnight, where you will have no problem finding the hits heard the previous evening during your trip to the nightclub!

❷ St James's Church★★

197 Piccadilly
☎ **0207 734 45 11**
Every day 8.30am-6.30pm.

Built by Christopher Wren in 1684, this charming church

osts the marriages of the
ondon gentry. A flea market
held here at the end of
ach week (Thu., Fri. and
at., 10am-6pm). You can
so benefit from the little
afé in the shadow of the
hurch (Café Nero ☎ 0207
37 9418, Mon.-Sat. 8am-
pm, Sun 10am-6pm, very
ood value and with its
wn terrace).

MacKenzie's★★

**69 Piccadilly
☎ 0207 495 55 14
Mon.-Sat. 9.30am-6pm,
Sun. 11am-5.15pm.**

ashes, sweaters, kilts, tartan
y the yard, everything to do
ith traditional Scottish
lothing which you could
ossibly dream of bringing
ack with you. It goes
ithout saying that the store
lso offers an exceptional
riendliness and gentility.

❹ The Royal Academy★★

**Burlington House
☎ 0207 300 57 60
Every day 10am-6pm
(Fri. 7.30pm).
Entry fee.**

This museum, every bit as
British as the Academy of Fine
Art, holds the largest temporary
exhibitions in the city. The one
held in the summer of the
year 2000 was the world's
largest ever exhibition of
contemporary art. It is
certainly worth the detour; its
program is displayed on the
façade (and in the subway). If
you don't have sufficient time

to devote to it, at least go and
see the *Madonna and Child*,
a marble sculpture by
Michelangelo.

❺ Fortnum and Mason's★★★

**181 Piccadilly
☎ 0207 734 80 40
Mon.-Sat. 10am-6.30pm,
Sun. 11am-5pm.
Tea served between 3pm
and 5.15pm.**

Liveried porters welcome every
visitor, whether they purchase
anything or not. Fortnum and
Mason's is most famous for its
blend of tea, now exported in
large quantities, but the
magnificent food department
is worth the trip. All the

English specialties are on offer.
The staff in the tearooms on
the fifth floor, dressed in style,
will serve you with care and
amiability.

❻ Burlington Arcade★★★

Here you are in cashmere
heaven: no less than five
boutiques! The best is without
doubt N. Peal at No. 71
(☎ 0207 493 0912, Mon.-Sat.
9.30am-6.00pm), which has
the largest range of different
colors and styles. If, in spite of
everything, you have no luck
here, try a visit to Berk at
No. 20-21 and 46-49 (☎ 0207
493 0028, Mon.-Fri. 9.00am-
5.30pm, Sat. 9.30am-5:30pm).
Don't miss The Irish Linen
Company at No. 35-36
(☎ 0207 493 89 49,
Mon.-Fri. 9.30am-5.45pm,

Sat. 10am-4.30pm, see p. 114) if you wish to sleep in the finest sheets in the world.

❼ Waterstone's★
203-206 Piccadilly
☎ 0207 851 24 00
❻ 0207 851 24 01
www.waterstone.co.uk
Mon.-Sat. 10am-10pm,
Sun. 12-6pm.

Several floors upon which to browse among the whole spectrum of English literature. Waterstone's is a huge bookstore where books of all genres are to be found. You will spend an enjoyable time leafing through any one of its numerous volumes in one of the reading areas placed at your disposal.

❽ Wedgwood★★★
173-174 Piccadilly
☎ 0207 629 26 14
Mon.-Fri. 9am-6pm,
Sat. 9.30am-6pm.

The famous dark blue Wedgwood porcelain is such a part of British heritage that it featured in a large retrospective exhibition at the Victoria and Albert Museum in 1995. The current collection of fine bone china offers a wide choice of designs, such as flowers and animals, and most of all ornaments of neo-classical or of oriental origin. In the same store you will also find Waterford, the celebrated Irish crystal, and the no less famous Coalport decorative plates.

❾ The Ritz★★★
Piccadilly
☎ 0207 493 81 81
Tea served at 1.30pm
(reservations not required)
3.30pm and 5.30pm
(reservations 15 days in advance)

Who has not dreamed of one day taking tea at the Ritz? To make your dream come true, you will need to make a reservation two weeks before your departure, but you won't regret it. Don't forget to dress smartly and bring a tie, although, if need be, one

may be borrowed from the cloakroom.

❿ Turnbull and Asser★★
71-72 Jermyn Street and 23 Berry Street
☎ 0207 808 30 00
Mon.-Fri. 9am-6pm,
Sat. 9.30am-6pm.

HRH The Prince of Wales is a patron of the house, a guarantee if not of good taste then at least of good sense and quality. Here you will find superb ready-to-wear shirts from £355. By contrast, at no. 23 Berry Street, a custom-made

THE CLUBS OF ST JAMES'S STREET

St James's Street boasts some of London's most exclusive clubs, the members of which are drawn from among the aristocracy. This is still very much a living tradition in England, and there are several dozen in the area, around The Mall and St James's Park. Men come here to eat, drink and talk among their equals; very few admit women. One of the most famous and most exclusive is Brook's (on the corner of St James's and Park Place). The Carlton Club, at no. 69, is the conservative stronghold. None of them admit tourists.

irt can be obtained for £110,
t you will have to buy six!

⓫ James Lock
nd Co★★★
St James Street
☎ 0207 930 88 74
on.-Fri. 9am-5.30pm,
at. 9.30am-5.30pm.

tering this store, one of the
ost famous of St James's
reet, will have you following
the footsteps of Brummell
ld of Lord Byron. Both were
ents here, as is today the
ince of Wales, and you will
putting yourself into friendly
ld expert hands if you want
buy a hat.

⓬ John Lobb★★★
St James's Street
☎ 0207 930 36 64
lon.-Fri. 9am-5.30pm,
at. 9am-4.30pm.

ven if you have neither the
ne nor the money to have
me shoes made (which

ome with a lifetime
uarantee), don't hesitate to
isit this store, which is
onsidered to be one of the
nest in the world. You can
lso admire the specialist
xpertise of the designers of
he house in the neighboring
tudio. Cast your eye also over
he mezzanine where all the

styles are presented on beautiful wooden displays.

⓭ Royal Doulton★★
167 Piccadilly Street
☎ 0207 493 91 21
Mon.-Sat. 9.30am-6pm.

It is primarily the porcelain
figurines, rivaling those of
Meissen, which has given Royal
Doulton its reputation for almost
two centuries. The best-known
models are the Fair Ladies, and
these make excellent gifts. You
will also find table pieces here.

⓮ Taylor of Old
Bond Street★★★
74 Jermyn Street
☎ 0207 930 53 21
Mon.-Sat. 8.30am-6pm.

The barber does not shave for

free, but it can be an amusing
experience to reconnect with
old methods of shaving,
whether on site or by buying
all the necessary items. The
house is also a specialist in
aromatherapy and herbalism.

Mayfair:
luxury, haute couture and antiques

Highly rated since the 18th century, Mayfair is today the center of the trade in luxury goods. Some of the best suppliers of antique art, such as the respected Colnaghi, are well established alongside great institutions like Sotheby's. If Old and New Bond Street form the heart of this walk, don't miss venturing down the neighboring streets, as well. South Molton Street, for example, is one of the prettiest pedestrian streets of the capital.

❶ Sotheby's★★
34-35 New Bond Street
☎ 0207 293 50 00
Mon.-Fri. 9am.-4.30 pm, some Sundays 12-4pm for special sales (reservations by telephone)

This is the oldest of London's auctioneers (1744), and the sworn enemy of the other great auction house, Christie's. All sales are conducted after a preliminary public viewing of lots (and are advertised in the published catalogs). Don't miss the Egyptian statue of the god Sekhmet dating from 1320 BC in the lobby.

❷ St George Hanover Square★★★
St George Street

This church is considered to be the most beautiful in the

est End, one of the finest xamples of Georgian rchitecture. Built in 1724, has played host to the omposer Handel, the arriage of the Shelleys (in 314) and the funeral of eorge Eliot (in 1880). side take a look at the ained-glass windows and the arms of George I.

Berkeley Square★

his square is bordered by

much appreciated for their practical elegance by active ladies. She has recently opened a restaurant in the store, which is very popular today.

❺ Vivienne Westwood Red Label★★★

44 Conduit Street
☎ **0207 439 11 09**
Mon.-Sat. 10am-6pm
(Thu. 7pm).

ome very beautiful esidences from the 18th entury. Take particular note f no. 44, at the corner of ill Tree and built in 1744; is considered to be one of he finest private mansions n London because of its umptuous interior. t night when the lamps re lit, you can appreciate the magnificent blue and gold eiling of the principal room.

❹ Nicole Farhi★★

58 New Bond Street
☎ **0207 499 83 68**
Mon.-Wed. 10am-6pm,
Thu. 10am-7pm, Sat.
10am-6.30pm.

This is the principal store of a British designer who blends style and comfort in clothes which are both classic and of good quality. Her suits are

One of the latest offspring of the Westwood boutiques, Red Label, her second line, is representative of the exuberance of the empress of punk: dresses of a provocative length (£250), sequined vests with excessive sleeves for men (£225), the designer's globe emblems to be worn as a pendant, and even cuff links.

❻ Smythson★★

44 New Bond Street
☎ **0207 629 85 58**
Mon.-Fri. 9.30am-6pm,
Sat. 10am-6pm.

The most highclass stationers in London, with extremely helpful staff. There is no need to have been born a Rothschild to buy yourself a present here; the writing paper is outstanding.

❼ Bond Street★★

124 New Bond Street
☎ **0207 351 53 53**
🖷 **0207 351 53 50**
Mon.-Sat. 10am-6pm.

This most chic of galleries specializes in antique silver and jewelry, but you can just as easily find porcelain here. The items are exceptional, with prices to match.
The address is prestigious, but you could come here simply to dream.

❽ Church's★★★

133 New Bond Street
☎ **0207 493 14 74**
Mon.-Sat. 9.30am-6pm
(Thu. 7pm).

A visit to Church's is a must for all men spending a weekend in London. This famous store sells a wide of shoes at reasonable prices.

But did you know that the brand also offers items for women of equally fine quality? For her, prices start at £80, although for men it is double that; however, it has been proven that their shoes are less likely to wear out than other brands.

⑨ Asprey★★★
169 New Bond Street
☎ 0207 493 67 67
Mon.-Fri. 10.30am-6pm, Sat. 10am-5pm.

Entering into this British temple of décor is somewhat intimidating. However, staff members are truly helpful and ready to assist you. So don't hesitate to push the

door open and go up to the second floor to take a look at the collection of English furniture from the 17th and 18th centuries, worthy of a museum of decorative arts. It also has a lovely collection of porcelain. No more expensive than anywhere else.

⑩ DKNY★★
27 Old Bond Street
☎ 0207 499 62 38
Mon.-Sat. 10.30am-6.30pm (Thu. 7pm), Sun. 12-6pm.

This New York designer store, providing comfortable clothes

for women, has an incredible internal architecture. The escalators look like something out of a science fiction movie. A café at the entrance and an "Absolutely Fabulous" clientele. But don't be fooled, you won't be pestered by the staff.

⑪ Jigsaw★
126 New Bond Street
☎ 0207 491 44 84
Mon.-Sat. 10am-6.30pm (Thu. 7.30pm).

Jigsaw, a franchised brand, offers clothing for all the family in original cuts and of an excellent quality.

THE CUSTOMER IS ALWAYS RIGHT

The shops in the area have the distinct privilege of supplying the local gentry, so you may find yourself face to face with staff somewhat, well, how can we put this, snobbish! Experience shows that in such a case you will need to be even haughtier. Finally don't forget that a unpleasant welcome is in any case a good reason for not buying anything.

...is magnificent store is ...mething of a showcase. ...th its seductive presentations ...d its wide choice, it has no ...ed to be envious of the ...xury stores next door, and its ...ices are reasonable (for ...ample £100 for a jacket).

) Paul Smith★★★
Avery Row
☎ 0207 493 12 87
on.-Sat. 10am-6pm
hu. 7pm).

...he collections for men from ...e two previous seasons are ...offer here at discounts of at ...ast 30 to 50 percent. Jeans ...art at £39, pants at £69, a ...it would cost £300, which is ...bout half the normal price. ...very good place to visit, ...ll not very well known.

) Browns★★
, 23-27, 38, 50 and 62
outh Molton Street
☎ 0207 491 78 33
on.-Sat. 10am-6.30pm
hu. 7pm).

...Browns had purchased the ...hole of South Molton Street, ...e situation could hardly be ...fferent: It occupies almost ...ery other store in this street. ...sells designer collections ...il Sander, Romeo Gigli, etc.), ...ut also its own line at no. 50. ...f note are the marked-down

designer clothes on the second floor of no. 38.

⑭ Claridges★★★
Brooks Street
☎ 0207 629 88 60.

Tea is served in the palace lobby daily at 3.00pm and 5.30pm. Pause a while in this noble institution and try one of the succulent gateaux. Don't even think of wearing jeans here, and straighten your tie before entering! You would be well advised to make a reservation.

⑮ The Guinea★
30 Bruton Place
☎ 0207 499 12 10
Mon.-Fri. lunch 12-3pm,
Mon.-Sat. dinner 6-11pm.

This is the best place in all Great Britain to try steak and kidney pie, but be early because this restaurant is very popular! However, don't panic if you arrive too late and the specialty of the house is sold out, you will still be able to have an enjoyable meal from among the traditional English dishes. It is less expensive for lunch.

4

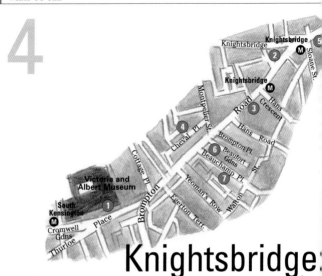

Knightsbridge
department stores and
luxury boutiques

Knightsbridge extends an invitation not just for
luxury shopping but also for the art of living.
So many treasures lie concealed within the
quietest streets. Just a few steps removed from
the lights of Harrod's you'll discover a thousand
temptations of both fashion and décor. To soak up
the atmosphere and trace the development of
costume and interior furnishings, refresh your
memory with a quick visit to the Victoria and
Albert Museum: It's right next door.

❶ Victoria and Albert Museum★★★

Cromwell Road
☎ 0207 942 20 00
Every day 10am-5.45pm,
Wed. and the last Fri. of
every month 10am-8pm.
Free entry

This exceptional museum of
decorative art, without doubt the
most elegant in the world, houses
items from Europe and from
former British colonies. If you are
short of time then don't miss

The Three Graces by Canova from
among all the treasures that it
contains; this has recently been
acquired by the museum (make
inquiries beforehand since the
sculpture is in Edinburgh for six
months of the year). But if you
have several hours to spare, at
least be sure to visit the Nehru
Gallery (Indian art from the
16th to the 19th centuries), the
costume galleries (a collection of
textiles from the 17th to the 20th
centuries) and the 20th-century
furniture gallery.

❷ Burberry★★★

2 Brompton Road
☎ 0207 806 13 16
or 0207 806 35 89
🖷 0207 434 26 20
www.burberry.com
Mon.-Sat. 10am-7pm,
Sun. 12-6pm.

It is impossible to miss the
Burberry brand with its little
check patterns on a background

leep beige. Lovers of classic
ade in England" fashions
ve never been disappointed by
e quality of its products, even
he range of garments has
en diversified over the years.
the midst of a collection of
usual" shirts, you will also
d everything necessary for
r four-legged companions.
ere is even an assortment of
lars with Burberry tartan
ds costing £99.

will be spoiled for choice on
the five levels of this store.

❹ Pandora★★★
16-22 Cheval Place
☎ **0207 589 52 89**
Mon.-Sat. 9am-6pm.

This dress agency offers
clothing from the great
couturiers for resale in
excellent condition.

❶ Harrod's★★★
-135 Brompton Road
0207 730 12 34
on.-Sat. 10am-7pm.

is impossible to leave this
ea without one of those
mous green and yellow
ags. Once inside, at least
eat yourself to a teddy bear,
r it is here in this huge store
at these soft toys are at their
veliest. Certainly do not fail
visit the famous Food Hall,
ith its immense range of
odstuffs, and for the rest you

Above all, you may touch
and try on anything and
everything without fear of
attracting scornful looks.
The little streets leading here
are worth a special visit in
themselves.

❺ Harvey Nichols★★★
109-125 Knightsbridge
☎ **0207 235 50 00**
www.harveynichols.com
Mon.-Sat. 10am-7pm
(Wed.-Thu.-Fri. 8pm),
Sun. 10am-6pm.

Take a free fashion tour in
front of Harvey Nichols's
windows and then join battle
within. But beware, the
cheapest T-shirt could cost
£50. Husbands and wives
can purchase matching
underwear, the ladies'
garments in smaller sizes.

Everything is classical and in
good taste. Unbeatable for its
overcoats and raincoats.

At £25, this is a must for style
and comfort.

❻ John Boyd/ Pamela★★
16 Beauchamp Place
☎ **0207 589 76 01**
Mon.-Fri. 10am-5pm,
Sat. by appointment

Here you will find two separate
shops run by the same
proprietor. In the first floor
window there is an admirable
assortment of hats for a special
evening occasion (starting at
£240). Branded formalwear is
to be found in the basement.

❼ BEAUCHAMP PLACE
This is one of the most chic
and fashionable streets.
The designer Caroline
Charles, at no. 56-57
(see p. 102), is couturier
to princesses. This could
be an attractive option
for you if you have the
money, in a setting more
evocative of the salon of
a private mansion than a
clothing store!

5

Chelsea:
down the King's Road

Twenty years ago, flaunting one's outfit along the King's Road was very much the done thing. The original punks loitered around the boutique of Vivienne Westwood and the trendy avant-garde jostled for position. Times have very much changed: The boutiques may still be following fashion but they are no longer setting it, and the King's Road, capitalizing on its success, has become a stylish street. This area is the occasion for a pleasant stroll and a favored rendezvous for Saturday afternoon shopping.

❶ King's Road★★★

At one time having fallen out of favor, King's Road has rediscovered its attractive and animated former self. Much frequented by Londoners, it is less overrun by tourists than Covent Garden, and less expensive than the luxury districts of Mayfair and Knightsbridge. This ancient route of kings includes two of the best stores for children in the city: Trotters (at no. 34, ☎ 0207 259 9620) and Daisy and Tom (at no. 181-183,

☎ 0207 352 5000) where you will certainly find gifts to bring lasting pleasure. Another good place to visit is Heal's (at no. 234, ☎ 0207 349 8411), this time dedicated to home and interiors.

❷ The Pheasantry★
152 King's Road.

Stop a while to admire the façade of this building. It was built in 1765, but a French family transformed it in 1881. The entrance porch is a copy of the Arc de Triomphe du Carrousel in Paris. Before becoming a restaurant, this address was a ballet school where Margot Fonteyn took her first steps.

Steinberg and Tolkien★★★

3 King's Road
0207 376 36 60
Mon.-Sat. 11am-7pm,
Sun. 12-6pm.

The in-crowd come to this wacky shop for an outfit costing a few pounds.

Here they will find costume jewelry, silks, satins, dresses, pumps and evening purses in the great tradition of glamor and glitter. A survivor of the best years of the King's Road, it has what it takes to cater for the most demanding.

❹ Mandy★★

39 King's Road
☎ 0207 376 74 91
Mon.-Sat. 10am-7pm,
Sun. 12-6pm.

For an evening out or to make an impression, and anyhow to be at the height of fashion, you've come to the right place. Satin trousers in all colors and small T-shirts that expose the midriff, here is the best store for clubwear in the whole street.

❺ World's End Vivienne Westwood★★★

430 King's Road
☎/☏ 0207 352 65 51
Mon.-Sat. 10am-6pm.

Here you are in Vivienne Westwood's premier store, where she founded the punk movement together with Malcolm McLaren. Bright red Mohicans and safety pins have

The Bibendum building (see p. 92) is one of the most spectacular in Chelsea.

disappeared, to be replaced by crowds of overseas tourists. Here you will find classic collections as well as jewelry and footwear. This boutique offers the colors that nowhere else does.

❻ Royal Avenue★

The foundations of this avenue were laid as far back as the end of the 17th century, when King William III wanted to connect his new residence at Kensington with the Royal Hospital. It has never surpassed the King's Road. Ian Fleming made it famous as the London address of James Bond.

❼ THE ROYAL HOSPITAL

This hospital is located on Royal Avenue. Conceived in 1682 by the great architect Christopher Wren, it offers permanent residence to 400 former soldiers. If you are in London during May, take advantage of the flower shows which take place in the gardens.

6

Leicester Square:
the entertainment distric

Eating Chinese, buying British at Burberry, listening to the voices of
angels at St-Martin-in-the-Fields, finding theater seats in Leicester
Square, all this you can do in the area located between Shaftesbury
Avenue and Trafalgar Square. Whether by day or by night, this is one
of the liveliest parts of the center of London, divided between the
exoticism of Chinatown and the so-British Nelson's Column.

❶ National Gallery★★★

Trafalgar Square
☎ 0207 747 28 85
Mon.-Sun. 10am-6pm,
Wed. 10am-9pm.
Free entry

The National Gallery is
much smaller than the
Louvre, and houses only the
masterpieces of European
painting from the 13th to
the beginning of the 20th
centuries, displayed in

chronological order.
Do not miss *The Baptism of
Christ* by Piero della

Francesca, Holbein's
The Ambassadors, the
Rembrandt rooms, *The
Rokeby Venus* by Velázquez,
or *The Bathers* by Cézanne.

❷ Trafalgar Square★★★

John Nash conceived this
monumental square during
the 1830s. It is dominated by
Nelson's column 56m (184ft)
high, atop which is the statue
of the celebrated admiral

who died in 1805 at the Battle of Trafalgar. Trafalgar Square has become a focal point for political rallies, electioneering and the revelers on New Year's Eve.

❸ St-Martin-in-the-Fields★★

Trafalgar Square
☎ 0207 766 11 00
Every day 8am-5pm;
service Sunday at 11.30am.

James Gibbs built this church in 1724. In contrast to other churches designed by the same architect, it is not influenced at all by the Baroque but rather by neo-classicism. Its architecture has been much copied. It contains a small craft market

(every day from 11am to 5pm, Sundays from noon), but it is for its famous vocal ensemble that this church is known the world over (reservations for concerts. ☎ 0207 839 83 62).

❹ Leicester Square★★

The brick façade of the Odeon, an enormous art-deco movie theater, dominates one of the best-known squares in London, almost entirely given over to entertainment, as confirmed by the two statues of Shakespeare and of Charlie Chaplin which have been erected here. A very practically minded kiosk sells off tickets here for theater performances: don't hesitate to try your luck. It is open between 2.30pm and 6.30pm, seats are generally at half price.

❺ Gerrard Street★★

Here is the heart of London's Chinatown. At no. 42-44, the Loong Fu supermarket sells exotic fruit and dishes. Stores selling comics and value tableware open their arms to you for that original gift. This

street is also the ideal place to eat Chinese at reasonable prices. The choice is yours!

❻ Burberry of London★★★

18-22 Haymarket
☎ 0207 930 33 43
Mon.-Fri. 10am-7pm,
Sun. 10am-6pm.

Practically guaranteed for life, a Burberry will outlive all fads and fashions. If the raincoats (at £300) leave you cold, cast an eye over the very good children's selection or resort to the sweaters: nothing but the best quality.

❼ THE NATIONAL PORTRAIT GALLERY

St Martin's Place
☎ 0207 306 00 55
Sat.-Wed. 10am-6pm,
Thu.-Fri. 10am-9pm.
Free entry
This offers a whirlwind tour of the history of Great Britain as seen through its principal characters: Kings, artists, heroes and villains, all those who made history since the 14th century are on display cheek by jowl, including Margaret Thatcher and Mick Jagger.

7

A few steps around Covent Garden

Even though the original market area has been preserved, Covent Garden has lost a large part of its authenticity. The pedestrianized streets and the boutiques have multiplied, like so many traps for your credit card. Today the ancient passages such as Neal's Yard lack their previous charm, beaten back by the soulless urbanization of the refurbished areas. However, in spite of this, Covent Garden is still one of the most pleasant places to go shopping. Avoid Sunday afternoons: Even though many stores are open, they are almost inaccessible because of the sheer number of tourists.

❶ London Transport Museum★★

The Piazza
☎ 0207 379 63 44
Sat.-Thu 10am-6pm,
Fri. 11am-6pm. Entry fee

Located in the old flower market, this museum traces the history of public transportation in London in a very pleasant venue. Don't miss the opportunity to sit in the driver's seat of a subway train or a double-decker bus. If you have children with you, they will love the interactive videos. In the shop near the exit, you can find plenty of fun gifts.

❷ The Royal Opera House★

Bow Street
☎ 0207 240 12 00.

Mahler directed Wagner in this building which dates from 1858. Today it houses the orchestra and the ballet of the Royal Opera which are

which have been transformed into an attractive shopping arcade, cafés and boutiques alternate and roving musicians add a touch of atmosphere. Don't miss The Candle Shop in the basement of Covent Garden's central courtyard (☎ 0207 379 4220, www.candlesontheweb.co.uk, open Mon.-Fri. 10am-7pm, Sat. 10am-8pm), or Benjamin Pollock's toyshop (at no. 44, ☎ 0207 379 7866, see p. 111).

th world-famous. You will
ve difficulty obtaining
kets, but some special
rformances are displayed
the big screen. Go there in
y case just to admire the
agnificent façade.

The Market★★★

outiques Mon.-Sat.
am-6pm.

the two floors of the
iginal vegetable market,

❹ Lush★★

The Piazza
☎ **0207 240 45 70**
📠 **0120 249 37 85**
www.lush.co.uk
Mon.-Sat. 10am-7pm,
Sun. 12-6pm.

Want a nice bath with bubbles and mousse? At Lush you will find everything you need to make your bathtub into a veritable little haven of peace. Between bath bombs such as the Sex Bomb, which is full of surprises, or tablets of gel soap, aficionados of the quick dip will certainly find something to make them happy.

❺ Buffalo★★

47-49 Neal Street
☎ **0207 379 10 51**
Mon.-Sat. 10.30am-7pm,
Sun. 12-5pm.

Buffalo is the original brand name of the platform shoes since copied by Morgan and No Name. The heels can be as high as 15cm (6in), but the excellent design of the shoes enables them to maintain their lightness and stability. Treat yourself to an explosive and way-out look (£100 for the most extravagant styles).

❻ Food For Thought★

31 Neal Street
☎ **0207 836 02 39**
Mon.-Sat. 9.30am-11.30am,
Sun. 12-5pm.

Relive the trend: "I eat bio, therefore I am." In this very fashionable vegetarian café–restaurant, you can have soup, pâté or salad drenched with carrot juice, sitting either among the crowd or in more intimate alcoves. Moreover you can give your eco-dietary conscience a boost for very little (approx. £5 per person).

❽ The Loft★
35 Monmouth Street
☎ 0207 240 38 07
Mon.-Sat. 11am-6pm
Sun. 12.45-4.45pm.

Are you looking for a Paul Smith suit, a Westwood jacket or just simply an original sweater? Don't have the means to buy? No problem: the first floor is full of affordable temptations for you, sir, while in the basement, madam, you will come across that black dress that you saw in *Elle* magazine. The type of place which will reunite you as a couple.

❾ Cenci★★★
31 Monmouth Street
☎ 0207 836 14 00
Mon.-Sat. 11am-6pm.

Sweaters and suits and sunglasses and shirts and shoes and purses. In brief, everything that could have been worn by your parents or your grandparents and which you never thought to preserve, even though you find that it suits you very well. A very congenial place but a little expensive for what it is.

❿ Black Out II★★
51 Endell Street
☎ 0207 240 50 06
Mon.-Fri. 11am-7pm,
Sat. 11.30am-5.30pm.

This is one of the best retro clothes stores in London, with stocks from the Roaring Twenties to the disco years. Reproduction dresses of the Hollywood queens (£65), but also shirts printed for th cousins of the Beach Boys (£20). Don't hesitate to descend on the overloaded racks to find that gem that you've always dreamed about.

⓫ Koh Samoui★★
65 Monmouth Street
☎ 0207 240 42 80
Mon.-Sat. 10.30am-6.30pm
Thu. 10.30am-7pm,
Sun. 11.30am-5.30pm.

Wood, steel, dried flowers an essential mirrors all blend successfully in this boutique which has established itself as one of the most importan distributors for young English designers. You may rest assured: There will be n risk of an office colleague wearing the skirt or blouse

❼ THE BOX
32-34 Monmouth Street
☎ 0207 240 58 28.
This fashionable bar attracts a very mixed clientele during the day, more gay by night. This is a truly convivial place; don't be afraid to cross the threshold and sit at one of the light wood tables to

take a break in a calm and relaxed atmosphere. Here you will have a ringside seat for observing the very latest trends.

at you have just bought
r about £200, as all the
les are original and
uasi-unique.

Screen Face★★
Monmouth Street
☎ 0207 836 39 55
0207 836 39 44
www.screenface.com
Mon.-Sat. 10am-7pm,
Sun. 12-5pm.

rofessional makeup from
oor to ceiling: from simple
ascara to the false eyelashes
the stars. Here you will
so find products for body
ainting (to turn yourself
mpletely green, for
xample). Very low prices,
nd free advice. The store's
esigners also work for
eatrical companies.

The Tea House★★★
5A Neal Street
☎ 0207 240 75 39
Mon.-Thu., Sat. 10am-7pm,
ri. 10.30am-7pm,
un. 12-6pm.

he red and black lacquered
ooden façade and décor
vite you on a journey

among the teapots. An
imaginary journey, of course,
but one of good quality since
you are just in the right place
here to discover the thousand

and one aspects of this cult
drink. Not a single flavor is
missing from among the
fabulous collection of house
teas, which includes some
originalities such as whisky
tea, rum tea or summer
pudding tea, at £2 per 125g
(4oz). Be sure to cast a good
eye over the unbelievable
collection of teapots, of every
shape imaginable.

⑭ Neal's Yard Dairy★★★
17 Shorts Gardens
☎ 0207 645 35 50
Mon.-Sat. 9am-7pm.

The cheeses of the house are
all either English or Irish,
produced sometimes in very
remote farms which can be
identified by the name
written on the rind. Without
any doubt these are not
pasteurized. The proprietors,
who opened the shop in
1979, are passionate about
giving advice, but you can
also take a chance and
purchase at random. If you
are a cheese lover this is a
fantastic store.

painted wall in Neal's Yard

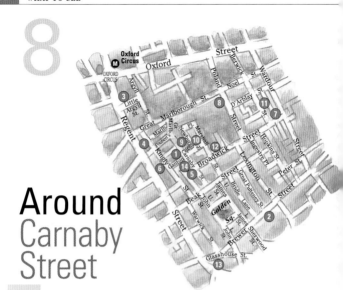

Around
Carnaby
Street

This part of Soho is one of the centers of London fashion. The latest designers have opened their boutiques here, next door to recognized brands. Ideal for trendy shopping at an unhurried pace.

❸ Laura Ashley★★
256-258 Regent Street
☎ 0207 437 97 60
Mon.-Tue. 10am-6.30pm, Wed., Fri. 10am-7pm, Thu. 10am- 8pm, Sat. 10am-7pm, Sun. 12-6pm.

❶ Carnaby Street★★
Today's souvenir shops are of little interest, but you must see this legendary street that led the pop world during the 1960s, at a time when the Beatles and the Stones competed for No. 1 place in the charts: This was one of the cult places of the hippie movement and of flower power. Today you will see mostly foreign teenagers, all nationalities being represented, taking a linguistic vacation.

❷ Brewer Street★
At no. 71 is the London address of the Knight of Eon. This legendary figure was dispatched by Louis XV of France to prepare an invasion of England which never took place. He remained in London for most of the rest of his life, widely talked about because of his eccentricities and especially because no one could be sure whether this was a man or a woman. As a consequence, perhaps, Brewer Street is today known mainly for its sex shops.

...is is the perfect address for ...rry-eyed young ladies or ...r those who, the epitome of ...inement, want to look like ...eir gardens. There is a sober ...d predictable style to be ...und here, collection after ...llection. Children's clothing ...every bit as orderly, and it ...ould not be the done thing to ...ow them to play in the ...ndpit or to do some painting ...wearing this brand.

⬤ Liberty★★★
...0-220 Regent Street
...0207 734 12 34
...on.-Wed. 10am-6.30pm
...hu. 8pm), Fri.-Sat. 10am-
...m, Sun. 12-6pm.

...berty, for all that it is not a ...rden, is nevertheless truly ...e kingdom of little flowers. ...erything you see inside the ...agnificent black wood ...terior is true to the tradition ... this famous brand.

Apart from the prints, there is also an elegant range of feminine fashions and of tableware. Above all, don't miss the half-timber mock Tudor façade in Great Marlborough Street.

❺ Muji★★★
41 Carnaby Street
☎ 0207 287 73 23
Mon.-Sat. 10am-7pm,
Sun. 12-6pm.

An obligatory stop! The décor of this boutique, with shelves and racks in light-colored wood, is typical of its household accessories and of its stationery, characterized by invisible lines and the use of recycled paper. Here you can acquire for a few pounds the pen that your boss will envy, the soap dish that will give your bathroom a look straight out of *Ideal Home*, in a word, unique articles of a much sought-after style. The sort of place that makes London the envy of the rest of Europe.

❻ Hamleys★★
188-196 Regent Street
☎ 0207 494 20 00
Mon.-Fri. 10am-8pm, Sat.
9.30am-8pm, Sun. 12-6pm.

Even if you don't have children, take a tour around this department store for toys and games, which is a tourist attraction in its own right because of its astonishing selection. Aficionados can also be enthralled by the Disney Store, at no. 140 (☎ 0207 287 6558, Mon.-Sat 10am-8pm, Sun. noon-6pm).

❼ Agent Provocateur★★★
6 Broadwick Street
☎ 0207 439 02 29
Mon.-Sat. 11am-7pm.

Are you always to be seen in your Bunny Yeager but lack the necessary accessories to complete your pinup fantasy? Fortunately, Agent Provocateur has arrived and, amid its boudoir interior, you can choose the bra to show off all your sex appeal.

❽ Yo! Sushi★★
52 Poland Street
☎ 0207 287 04 43
Every day noon-midnight.

It matters not that the sushi isn't quite orthodox, this restaurant is the ultimate experience in cyber-dinners. You sit around a high-tech counter in order to seize on whichever dishes take your fancy from among those revolving in front of you, and which vary in price according to color. R2D2's little brother will serve your drinks. As for ambience, three screens constantly broadcasting MTV leave little room for amorous confidences.

❾ The Dispensary★
8 Newburgh Street
☎ 0207 287 81 45
Mon.-Sat. 10.30am-6.30pm
Sun. 12-5pm.

Two addresses in the same street, one for men and the other for women. In each you will also find a children line completely in denim, very successfully done. A very trendy look for young as well as old, with T-shirts of a Japanese design at the right price.

Jess James★★
Newburgh Street
0207 437 01 99
Mon.-Sat. 11am-6.30pm
Thu. 7pm).

...u may wish to embellish the ...fit that you have just ...quired from the above-...ntioned address with a ...acelet or ring of an equally ...uristic design, such as those ... offer in this boutique of ...perb window displays. It ...uld be said that once having ...lked down Newburgh Street ...u will soon pass for an avid ...ader of *Dazed and Confused* ...ee p. 125).

Nico Didonna★★
Berwick Street
0207 287 02 07
...ery day 11am-7pm.

...co Didonna is a new stylist ... men's fashions. Simple ...signs, effective and very ...endy. Handpainted T-shirts ...st £35, and for a pair of ...ants of an original style ...orthy of Soho you must ...unt on paying between £80 ...nd £218. All designs are ...iginal and quasi-unique.

Contemporary ...eramics★
Marshall Street
: 0207 437 76 05
Mon.-Sat. 10.30am-6pm
Thu. 7pm).

This boutique showcases the work of British master potters. In the bay windows it is possible to see everything which is on sale: tableware, vases and jewelry. Many pieces are original creations but the prices remain very modest.

⑬ Aquascutum★★
100 Regent Street
☎ 0207 675 82 00
Mon.-Sat. 10am-6.30pm
(Thu. 7pm), Sun. 12-5pm.

Upper-middle-class British style is predominant in this virtual department store which offers masculine and feminine fashions in a sanitized environment of dominant white and gold. Nothing revolutionary, the clientele is rather of a certain age but staff members are friendly, and this is a very good location to buy a raincoat.

⑭ Rugbyscene★
46 Carnaby Street
☎ 0171 439 07 78
Mon.-Sat. 10am-7pm.

Rugby is one of the most popular sports in Britain. At Rugbyscene, regular players as

REGENT STREET

If you wish to extend your stroll or are interested in tableware, then don't hesitate to walk along the entire length of Regent Street: in addition to the clothing and toy stores mentioned above, you will also find several boutiques selling porcelain, among them Lawley's at no. 154 (☎ 0207 734 3184). This store has massive chinaware sales in mid-January and mid-June. All brands are available and prices are as low as in the factory. Also see Kings of Sheffield, at no. 319 (☎ 0207 637 9888) for very good silverware. Ideal for making lots of purchases in a short space of time.

well as amateurs have at their disposal all the accessories necessary to become perfect little rugby players. The range of jerseys is impressive and it is possible to find here the strips of some teams completely unheard of outside Britain. Even if you have never seen the sport, the jerseys are fashionable. Connoisseurs will love it.

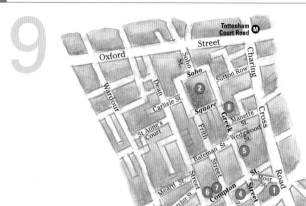

Around
Old Compton Street

For several years Old Compton Street has been London's new offbeat and fashionable center. A stronghold of the gay community, this street is the place to go in order to be seen and to feel the pulse of trendy London. Go to any of its numerous bars to find out about upcoming parties. It is in this area that you'll find the best tea in the city, so take a seat and watch the world go by: You'll be witnessing the (occasionally still) birth of avant-garde London. And so the show goes on.

❶ The Palace Theatre★

Shaftesbury Av.
☎ 0207 434 09 09.

This is one of the many theaters which punctuate Shaftesbury Avenue. This street is in fact almost entirely dedicated to entertainment houses: There are no less than eight, of which two are movie theaters. The Palace Theatre has the most interesting façade of them all. Its most luxurious interior is only open during a performance.

❷ Soho Square★

Take a breather in this pretty garden embellished with a charming little Tudor-style house which was built here during the

torian era. This square has
g been much sought after.
ok for example at no.10, a
h-century mansion that
ars witness to the past
endor of the area. At no. 2,
ybody suffering from Beatle-
nia may go and meditate
usly in front of Paul
Cartney's original office.

Ann Summers★★

Wardour Street
☎ 0207 434 24 75
on.-Sat. 10am-11pm,
n. 11am-10pm.

is store is part of a chain
ling sexy underwear and
cessories. Here you will find
travagant lingerie of
bious (but comical) taste,
well as gadgets such as a
cket Kamasutra (£5.99).

American
etro★★

5 Old Compton Street
☎ 0207 734 34 77
on.-Fri. 10.30am-19.30am,
at. 10.15am-7pm.

place of original
ccessories for gays and
ashion victims. On the first
oor are trendy masculine
lothes (W&LT, the Belgian
echno-designer), fantasy
ewelry, postcards, art books;
n the basement, household
ccessories both playful and
olorful. Lots of original
deas for gifts.

⑤ Kokon to Zai★★★

57 Greek Street
☎ 0207 434 13 16
Mon.-Sat. 11am-8pm,
Sun. 12-6pm.

A small shop, but the height
of international trends: house
music CDs limited to 20 copies,
the latest Nike trainers
imported from the US, and
famous European and Japanese
designers of tomorrow. The
stock is renewed twice as fast
as the wind. A must for show-
offs but beware, this comes
at a price.

⑥ Algerian
Coffee Shop★★

52 Old Compton Street
☎ 0207 437 24 80
Mon.-Sat. 9am-7pm.

The windows are chock-full of
teapots, coffeepots, packets of
coffee and tea, all very typical
of the contents of the store.
The interior is antiquated and
with a curious assortment of
disparate objects, but the best

coffees and teas in all London
are on sale.

⑦ Pâtisserie
Valérie★★★

44 Old Compton Street
☎ 0207 437 34 66
Mon.-Fri. 7.30am-10pm, Sat.
8am-8pm, Sun. 9am-6pm.

An island of good sense and
good taste, almost incongruous
within the ocean of eccentricity
which is Old Compton Street,
this venue is one of the best
for sampling French pastry
and for lovingly enjoying a
generous cappuccino.

⑧ Milroy's Soho
Wine Market★★

3 Greek Street
☎ 0207 437 93 11
Every day 10am-8pm.

All the whiskeys imaginable
are on sale here. The staff
members are admirable
at explaining the subtle
differences between the
hundreds of brands available.

THE BEST LOCAL CAFÉS

The Old Compton Café,
at no. 34, has a gay
clientele, its terrace is very
popular and it is open 24
hours a day. Balans, at no.
60, is scarcely less
crowded. Freedom, two
steps away at no. 60

Wardour Street, is one of the most fashionable
addresses, while the nostalgia for New York yuppie bars
can be assuaged at Mezzo, no. 100, a model of the genre.

10

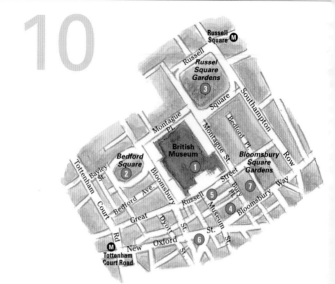

Around the
British Museum

The shadow of the British Museum dominates this corner of Bloomsbury, a favorite haunt of intellectuals and artists. Once it was Virginia Woolf or T. S. Eliot, nowadays it could be the likes of filmmaker Isaac Julian that you see just around the corner. Silence please, students working! – in the library of the British Museum or at the University of London close by. Now it's your turn to concentrate your mind, whether in the gardens, standing in front of the façades, or simply in choosing your next sweater!

❶ British Museum★★★
Great Russell Street
☎ 0207 636 15 55
Mon.-Tue. 10am-5pm, Thu.-Fri. 10am-8.30pm, Wed.-Sat. 10am-5pm, Sun. 12-6pm.
Free entry

Take some time out at the British Museum. There are good reasons why it is more visited than the Louvre in Paris or the Metropolitan Museum of New York. The Rosetta Stone, thanks to which Champollion succeeded in deciphering hieroglyphics, is a must. It is situated near the entrance. Be sure to visit also the Egyptian antiquities (magnificent mummies) as well as the Parthenon sculptures which the Greeks still claim today.

before leaving, don't forget the museum shop where you will find interesting reproductions.

● Bedford Square★★

At the entrances to the buildings lining this elegant Georgian square (1775) are decorated with artificial stone. This square, belonging to the Duke of Bedford, is one of the numerous estates of which London is composed.

Halicarnassus, and the statue of the highly unpopular King George I overlooking it are perhaps the cause of this.

● Westaway and Westaway★★

65 Great Russell Street
☎ 0207 405 44 79
Mon.-Sat. 9.30am-6pm.

This store may smell somewhat of mothballs and its staff may appear a little old-fashioned, but it is undoubtedly the best address in terms of both quality and price for woolens and tartans for all the family. The selection is certainly not as broad as elsewhere, particularly

● Russell Square Gardens★★

Here, sitting on one of the benches in the gardens, you can admire some of the most beautiful Victorian houses in London.

● St George's Bloomsbury★

Bloomsbury Way
☎ 0207 405 30 44
Mon.-Fri. 9.30am-5.30pm,
Sun. 9am-5pm, service
Sun. at 10.30am.

This church, built by N. Hawksmoor for the wealthy inhabitants of the district, has always aroused criticism and ridicule. Its north-facing mock-Renaissance façade, its pyramidal bell tower which was inspired by the Mausoleum at

in terms of colors which tend to the very quiet, but the Shetland you can buy here (£35–£50) will not wear out as quickly.

● James Smith and Sons★★★

53 New Oxford Street
☎ 0207 836 47 31
Mon.-Fri. 9.30am-5.30pm,
Sat. 10am-5.30pm.

Smith and Sons is quite simply the finest umbrella store that you could possibly imagine. Still with its original décor (dating from 1857), the thousands of umbrellas here will make the drizzle worthwhile. For good weather, traditional walking sticks or, rather more unusual, parasols with automatic handles are most striking.

● PIED BULL YARD

This is a charming passageway between Bloomsbury Square Gardens and Bury Place where you will find stores selling photographic equipment (one of the specialties of the area) and Truckles, a pleasant café with a summer terrace. A few paces further, while browsing among the antiquarian bookstores in Museum Street, think of Charles Dickens, Virginia Woolf and T. S. Eliot, all of whom lived around here.

Oxford Street:
the place to shop

When you arrive at Oxford Street you get the impression that the whole world has arranged to meet here. The sidewalks, however wide, are often choked by crowds surging from boutique to department store. Don't give in to that feeling of being drained – here you are at the heart of London shopping. A friendly word of advice: The streets nearby, such as Christopher's Place, are much more peaceful, and it is there you will find a little café or simply a place to rest and regain your equilibrium.

❶ Wallace Collection★★★

**Herford House,
Manchester Square
☎ 0207 935 06 87
Mon.-Sat. 10am-5pm,
Sun. 12-5pm. Free entry**

On entering the distinguished former mansion of Sir Richard Wallace (the original owner of the Château de Bagatelle, in the Bois de Boulogne in Paris), you can leave the frenetic consumerism of Oxford Street behind you. The widow of this collector bequeathed all his works of art to the people of Great Britain. They have been displayed ever since in this beautiful residence. The collection of French paintings from the 18th century is one of the finest in the world, with notable works by Watteau, Boucher and Fragonard.

❷ Speaker's Corner★★

Hyde Park, Sun. afternoon.
A little way off from Oxford Street you may witness one of the most astonishing of London's traditions. Every week since 1872, at the corner of Hyde Park, public speakers take the spotlight. Everybody is free to say what they feel on whatever subject they hold

ar. On the other side of
yde Park, Kensington
ardens and Palace are
orth seeing.

Marks & Spencer★
58 Oxford Street
0207 935 79 54
on.-Fri. 9am-9pm, Sat.
30am-8pm, Sun. 12-6pm.

ou will find one of these
ores just about everywhere.
he clothing here is of good
uality and inexpensive
ingerie, underwear, woolens,
c.). Even the school
niforms, which enjoy an
qually good reputation,
uld easily be put to good
se by a fashion victim with
little imagination. The
npeccable range of foodstuffs
very varied and of quite good
alue. A real prize.

Selfridges★★
00 Oxford Street
0870 837 73 77
on.-Fri. 10am-8pm, Sat.
30am-8pm, Sun. 12-6pm.

Because it is nicknamed
"the poor man's Harrod's" it
doesn't mean that Selfridges is
not worth a visit. Located in a
superb art-nouveau building,
it offers a wide variety of
products, clothing as well as
household accessories. Its low-
budget fashion line, Miss
Selfridge, offers a panorama
of the latest trends for just a
few pounds. If you find the
same item cheaper elsewhere,
Selfridges will refund your
purchase!

❺ St Christopher's Place★★★
This is one of the nicest
pedestrianized zones of
London, with a wide variety of
stores: Whistles, at no. 20-21,
has collections by young and
very gifted designers (such as
Sonja Nuttal) at affordable
prices. Buckle My Shoe, at no.
19, has London's largest
selection of children's shoes
(see p. 110).

❻ John Lewis★
278-306 Oxford Street
☎ 0207 629 77 11
Mon.-Fri. 10am-8pm,
Sat. 9.30am-6pm.

John Lewis's notions range is
famous throughout the whole
of London. Here you will find
everything you need to make
or alter your own apparel.
This store is the darling of
London because of its
unbeatable prices.

A LITTLE BIT OF GREENERY

Away from the bustle
of Oxford Street, go and
take a walk in Hyde
Park. This typically
English park extends at
its western end into
Kensington Gardens.
Also don't forget to
visit Kensington Palace,
former residence of
Princess Margaret.

12

A walk
in the City

The City of London is above all a business person's preserve. But don't panic, they are very well mannered. In order to meet the motley group of brokers, exchange dealers and financiers, don't let yourself be satisfied by a mere visit to the Tower and St Paul's. Some of the well-concealed pubs and cafés will give you a feel for the area much better than any organized tour. Of course this will take longer and involve going on foot. Note: This walk should only be done during the week.

has been used as a royal residence and above all as a prison. You can be assured of the shivers in Martin Tower where instruments of torture are on display.

❶ Tower of London★★★

Tower Hill
☎ 0207 709 07 65
Mar.-Oct., Mon.-Sat. 9am-6pm, Sun. 10am-6pm;
Nov.-Feb. Tue.-Sat. 9am-5pm, Sun.-Mon. 10am-5pm.
Entry fee. Disabled access

At the exit from the subway, the Tower looks like an impregnable citadel. It was built in 1097 to protect London against potential invaders. In the absence of assailants, it

❷ St Paul's Cathedral★★★

Ludgate Hill
☎ 0207 236 41 28
Mon.-Sat. 8.30am-4pm;
visits to the dome 9.30am-4pm. No visits Sun.,
but service at 10.30am.
Entry fee

Following the destruction of the original cathedral during the Great Fire of London in 1666, Christopher Wren was arged with its construction. He was spired by the plan of e dome of St Peter's in ome. Inside, climb to the hispering Gallery, so called cause the echo rries the

the two great gray-stone towers, only a short distance away from the Tower of London, you can visit a museum (entry fee) which traces the history of its creation and details one of the best-known monuments in the City of London.

❹ Leadenhall Market★★★
Whittington Av.

Mon.-Fri. 7am-4pm.

Some food trade is still conducted within the superb Victorian hall built in 1881 (poultry and game), but the clothing stores have gained ground.

❺ Saint Katharine's Docks★★★

At the foot of Tower Bridge, St Katharine's Docks make for a pleasant stroll. During the summer, the "white collar" workers of the City come here to remove their jackets and get a suntan over a sandwich during their lunch break. This little port still contains a few pleasure boats and pretty

wooden two-masters. A charming spot amid all the high-rise buildings.

❻ The Jamaica Wine House★★
Saint Michael's Alley
☎ 0207 929 69 72
Mon.-Fri. 11am-11pm.

This was the first coffee house to open in London, in 1652. The windows have the look of a small museum about them, with their old checks and dusty bottles. Very strict rules apply at the door: no entry without a tie. This is a place for the initiated only.

und of your voice all round the dome.

❷ Tower Bridge★★
ower Bridge
☎ 0207 403 37 61
☎ 0207 357 79 35
www.towerbridge.org.uk
very day 9.30am-6pm.

ower Bridge has spanned the hames since 1894, allowing assage over the river which vides London in two. Within

THE CROWN JEWELS

The same hours as the Tower of London. Entry fee

These can be admired without risk of getting tired since a moving walkway has been installed to stop visitors spending too much time in front of them! Virtually all the royal insignia were destroyed by Cromwell after the establishment of the Republic, and those which you see today in one of the rooms of the Tower of London date from the coronation of Charles II (1661). Don't miss either the crown of Queen Elizabeth or the enormous diamond of the royal scepter.

13

South Bank and the Tate Modern

This long walk will require an entire day, longer if you wish to linger in the Tate Modern. Don't miss either Shakespeare's Globe, which will transport you back to the 17th century, or the London Eye, which will give you a wonderful aerial view of London. Finally, escape from it all and dive headfirst into the ocean depths at the London Aquarium.

❶ Shakespeare's Globe★★

21 New Globe Walk
Bankside
☎ 0207 401 99 19
www.shakespeares-globe.org

This large wooden building with a thatched roof is a faithful reconstruction of the Globe, the theater for which Shakespeare wrote his greatest plays. The original theater, which was located nearby,

was in service until 1642. From May until September, performances take place in the open air of Shakespeare's works, naturally, but also concerts of classical music.

❷ Tate Modern★★★

Bankside
☎ 0207 887 80 08
www.tate.org.uk
Sun.-Thu. 10am-6pm,
Fri-Sat. 10am-10pm.
Free entry to the museum, entry fee for exhibitions

The Tate Modern was created with the goal of offering a place for exhibiting 20th century works of art previously shown at the Tate Gallery, now Tate Britain. The Bankside Power Station, with its unique architecture (by Sir Giles Gilbert Scott) and its extensive area, was an obvious choice. The Swiss architects Herzog and de Meuron respected the original construction when adding

...o more levels, which provide ...om for exhibitions and seven ...oors of galleries in total. In ...n interesting approach, the ...splays are organized by ...eme. The impressive Turbine ...all 155m (500ft) long and ...5m (110ft) high receives ...orks of corresponding ...roportions. At present you can ...e four sculptures by Louise ...ourgeois and, over the next ...ve years, there will be a ...uccession of different artists. ...truly unique venue.

...) Millennium ...ridge★

...ankside.

...he Millennium Bridge, built ...y Foster and Caro, joins St ...aul's Cathedral with the Tate ...odern. This pedestrian bridge ...f futuristic design is the first ...ridge over the Thames to

...ave been built for over a ...entury. There was a kind of ...rony in the fact that it had to ...e closed after its first day as it ...vas bending under the weight ...f visitors! But rest assured, it ...vas only a matter of time ...efore the experts found a ...vay to stabilize it.

❺ British Airways London Eye★★★

Bankside
☎ 0870 500 06 00
www.ba-londoneye.com
Apr.-Oct. 9am-8pm,
Nov.-Mar. 10am-4pm.
Entry fee (reservations
necessary in peak season)

Here you will find yourself standing in front of the biggest Ferris wheel in the world. At 135m (443ft) high, it is also the fourth tallest building in the capital. Provided you don't suffer from vertigo, climb aboard one of its 32 glass cabins and relax for a pleasant half hour. You will have a field of view extending to 40km (25 miles) on a clear day: the most spectacular view in the whole of London.

❻ London Aquarium★★

Southbank
☎ 0207 967 80 00
Every day 10am-6pm.
Entry fee

The London Aquarium, one of the largest in Europe, is a wonderful venue for young and old alike. On three levels, you will find over 100 varieties of marine plants and animals from all around the world. And above all, don't miss the most impressive tenants, the sharks.

❹ ROYAL NATIONAL THEATRE★★★

Southbank
Waterloo Tube
☎ 0207 452 34 00.

One of the largest theaters in the city (it actually houses three), the RNT has a wide choice of performances, from musical comedies to contemporary pieces. If you go during the summer, you can take part in open-air shows.

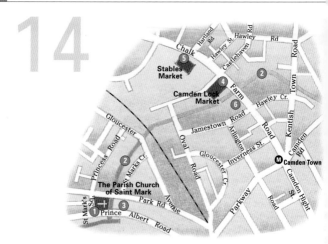

14

Stables Market
Camden Lock Market
The Parish Church of Saint Mark
Camden Town

Camden:
a touch of eccentricity

London's benchmark for everything secondhand, this giant flea market attracts a motley crowd and runs alongside the old canals of London. To reach it you don't have to take the subway. If you feel like a pleasant and peaceful stroll, cross Regent's Park and discover Camden by the water's edge.

❶ The Parish Church of St Mark★★★

Saint Mark's Square
☎ 0207 586 16 94
Eucharist:
Fri. 11am, Sun. 8am;
hymns: Sun. 10.30am;
requiem: Thu. 6.30pm.

After crossing Regent's Park, the little church of St Mark with its stained-glass rose window is an ideal spot to call a halt. And even if the Parish Church of St Mark is not always open to the public, the flower gardens with their shady benches are a veritable haven of peace prior to a little stroll along the canals leading to Camden.

❷ The canals of Camden★★

Following the canal which connects Regent's Park with Camden is one of the most enjoyable walks the capital has to offer. Wander along by the

stream and enjoy the sight of the little London barges. And if you wish to know more about the vibrant history of the canals of London, then continue your way alongside

e water as far as the
ndon Canal Museum
2-13 New Wharf Road,
☎ 0207 713 0836,
   0207 689 6679,
ww.canalmuseum.org.uk;
e.-Sun. 10am-4.30pm).

Feng Shang★★
umberland Basin, Prince
lbert Road
☎ 0171 485 81 37
☎ 0171 267 29 90.

aving crossed the little
angway which leads to the
ridge, Feng Shang invites its
ustomers onto a two-story
ed Saigon barge. Here you
an enjoy very good meals in
 grand style. The menu is
ot excessively expensive
between £22 and £42).
: also offers à la carte
ishes. The chicken satay
s particularly delicious.

❹ Camden Lock Market★★★
amden Lock has been one of
ondon's most popular
narkets for almost 25 years.
t's worth going there just for
his! On the former banks of
ne Regent's Canal locks,
undreds of small boutiques
ell all manner of things:
ewelry and clothing, new
or secondhand. You will also
ind unusual gifts here. But
oe sure to observe the local
nhabitants, too.

❺ Cyberdog★★
**Stables Market,
Chalk Farm Road
☎ 0207 836 78 55
www.cyberdog.co.uk
Fri-Sun. 10am-6.30pm.**

Even if you find the clothing
offered at Cyberdog completely
unwearable, the totally cyber-
style collection is certainly
worth a look. In the
underground galleries of this
techno store, the salespeople
from another dimension
sometimes look at you with a

disquieting eye. For £40, the
most adventurous "clubbers"
can carry off one of their
T-shirts with holographic
images.

❻ Starbucks★★
**Camden High Street,
Suffolk Wharf
www.starbucks.com**

Starbucks – originally an
American company – is

now one of the largest
coffeehouse chains in
Britain. In Camden, this
establishment is more like a
tourist center. Drinking a
cappuccino flavored with
chocolate, vanilla or
ground hazelnut, you can
glance over the history of
London transport displayed
on the walls. To go with
your coffee break choose
one of the many cheesecakes
on offer, a typically English
dessert.

BOATS★★

It isn't only possible to visit London on foot, by car, on
a bus or in the subway, you can also discover the
capital from another angle: by boat, traveling along the
canals. An ideal occasion to take the time to relax for a
day or two. The daintily decorated little wooden barges
are available either for guided tours or to rent.
Details from:

British Waterways Company:
☎ 0192 320 11 20 or www.britishwaterways.co.uk

Buckingham Palace

George IV and the royal architect, John Nash, transformed this former 18th-century manor house. Ever since the accession of Queen Victoria in 1837, it has been the official residence of British sovereigns. A royal flag flying above the building tells you that Her Majesty is in residence.

Visiting the Palace

Ever since a fire destroyed a part of Windsor Castle in 1992, about 20 of the 660 existing rooms of Buckingham Palace have been open to the public. Queen Elizabeth decided to open her residence for two months in the summer to help finance the rebuilding of the castle. The tour is confined primarily to the "staterooms." You will go through, in order, the Guardroom, the Grand Gallery and the Throne Room with the seats used during the coronation of Queen Elizabeth at Westminster in 1953.

The Queen's Gallery

This regularly displays the rich collection of works of art belonging to the Royal family, notably canvases by Vermeer and Leonardo da Vinci.

The Changing of the Guard

The ceremony of the Changing of the Guard of the Palace takes place every day at 11.30am in spring and summer, and every other day in fall and winter. The arrival of the advancing guard at the north gate signals the ceremonial handing over of the keys by the retiring guard.

His departure is marked by the sound of drums and fanfares. The ceremony is quite imposing and lasts about three-quarters of an hour.

INFORMATION

The Mall (see p. 38)
Tube: Green Park,
St. James's Park
☎ 0207 321 22 33
Entry fee
Rooms open every day
Aug.-Sep. 9am-4.30pm.
Changing of the Guard
at 11.30am every day
Apr.-Aug.; every other
day Sep.-Mar.

Westminster Abbey

The remains of a Benedictine monastery gave the name Westminster to one of the best-known districts of London. The original church was founded in the 11th century on the ruins of the "Monastery of the West," then rebuilt during the 13th century on the orders of Henry III and completed in the 14th century. The Abbey is both royal burial ground and site of coronations.

The Chapel of St. Edward the Confessor

Here you will find the tomb of the sainted king but above all the throne of oak used since 1308 for the coronation of the British monarchs. Beneath here lies the Stone of Scone which was used at the accession of the Scottish kings of the Middle Ages.

The nave

This may appear disproportionate, at 10.5m (34ft) wide and 31m (102ft) high. Its construction took 150 years. Near the entrance has stood the tomb of the Unknown Warrior since 1926. Not far from there is a tombstone to the memory of Churchill and the grave of the explorer Livingstone.

The north and nouth transepts

At the north end, the "Statesmen's Corner" houses the statues of famous politicians such as Disraeli and Gladstone. At the south end, the "Poet's Corner" contains the tombs of Dickens, Kipling and even of the actor Laurence Olivier. Shakespeare, buried in Stratford-upon-Avon, has a monument all to himself.

The sanctuary

The monarchs are crowned by the Archbishop of Canterbury between the transepts and behind the choir. Note the mosaic dating from the 13th century.

INFORMATION

Broad Sanctuary
(see p. 38)
Tube: Westminster
☎ 0207 222 5152
Nave and transepts:
Mon.-Sat. 8am-6pm,
Wed. 8am-7.45pm,
Sun. between services
Chapel: Mon.-Wed. 9am-
4.45pm, Sat. 9am-5.45pm
Entry fee, last entry one
hour before closing

Westminster Palace

A royal residence in the 11th century, the history of the palace has been determined by the different fires which have ravaged it. The first, in 1513, marked the departure of King Henry VIII for Whitehall and the establishment of the parliamentarians in what were still the ruins of the palace chapel. The second, in 1834, gave rise to the Parliament of today.

since 1958. Decisions undertaken look primarily to matters of constitution. Sessions are presided over by the Lord Chancellor who is also the Minister of Justice.

Big Ben

The real name of this famous London landmark is the Clock Tower. The nickname "Ben" refers to the builder Benjamin Hall and in fact designates the 14-tonne bell which, ever since 31 May 1859, has sounded every 15 minutes.

Victoria Tower

Higher than the Clock Tower, it is most famous for the passing of the Queen once a year. It is through here that the sovereign passes before entering the House of Lords to give the Queen's Speech which marks the opening session of Parliament.

The House of Commons

Sitting face to face, the members of the government are on the right and the opposition on the left. In the middle, the Speaker is charged with presiding over the parliamentary sessions. It is to him or her that the members must address their remarks, and not to other members.

The House of Lords

Of hereditary origin, life peerages have been conferred

INFORMATION

Parliament Square
(see p. 39)
Tube: Westminster
☎ 0207 219 3000
Mon.-Thu. 9am-6pm,
Fri. 4.30pm
House of Commons
(Nov.-end Jul.)
☎ 0207 219 4372
Mon.-Tue. and Thu.
from 2.30pm
Wed. 9.30am-3pm
(telephone in advance)
House of Lords
☎ 0207 219 3107
Mon.-Wed. from
2.30pm, Thu. from 3pm

National Gallery

Established in 1824 following the acquisition of 38 paintings from a financier of Russian origin, Parliament soon decided to allocate regular funds for the purchase of other master canvases. Due to lack of space, the works of art are presented in chronological order and exhibited by rotation.

Sainsbury Wing, 1260–1510

The most notable works of the Italian and Flemish schools are *The Virgin and Child* with *Saint Anne and Saint John the Baptist* by Leonardo da Vinci, *The Arnolfini Portrait* by Van Eyck and *The Doge Leonardo Loredan* by Bellini. This section of the museum, inaugurated in 1991, saw the light of day thanks to funds donated by Sainsbury supermarkets, hence the name.

West Wing, 1510–1600

Italian and German Renaissance works are the most represented here. Not to be missed are: Holbein (*The Ambassadors*), Michelangelo (*The Entombment* and *The*

Manchester Madonna), Titian (*Bacchus and Ariadne*) and el Greco (*Christ Driving the Traders from the Temple*).

North Wing, 1600–1700

Here again, it is impossible to describe all the wonders of this gallery. Our preferences would be for the pictures by Van Dyck (*Equestrian Portrait of Charles I*), Rubens, Vermeer (especially the canvas of *A Young Woman Seated at a Virginal*), and also Caravaggio.

East Wing, 1700–1920

The East Wing is the most recent in the National Gallery. Worth seeing for its works by Cézanne, Van Gogh, Seurat and Turner.

INFORMATION

Trafalgar Square
(see p. 52)
Tube: Leicester
Square,
Charing Cross
☎ 0207 747 2885
Mon.-Sat. 10.30am-6pm
Wed. until 9pm
Sun. 12 noon-6pm,
except Public
Holidays

Trafalgar Square

The name of this square is evocative: the immense fountains and Nelson's Column make this an essential walk which tourists will inevitably immortalize on film. The famous pigeons, which used to abound, have largely disappeared – thanks to concerted efforts by the authorities. Located in the heart of the capital, this is a busy square just as much used by Londoners themselves.

History in the making

Originally housing the royal stables of Whitehall, it wasn't until 1820 that the architect John Nash began the construction of the square as part of the works encompassing the development of the area around Westminster. Completed in 1840, it is today a point of rendezvous for political rallies and annual gatherings such as at New Year or the ceremony for installing of the Christmas tree traditionally donated by the Norwegians to the English, in remembrance of sacrifices made during World War Two.

Nelson's Column

The square would not be what it is without the monument erected in 1842 in honor of the admiral killed during the famous Battle of Trafalgar against Napoleon. The 56-m (150-ft) high granite monument with its 5.5-m (20-ft) high bronze statue commemorates British naval supremacy during the 19th century.

The church of St.-Martin-in-the-Fields

The church stands at the northeast corner of the square. It has been here since the 13th century but it owes its current design to James Gibbs who completed the work in 1726. Its anti-Baroque style has since inspired many architects in America. Inside, you will see the box in the gallery to the left of the choir for the use of the Royal family, since we are here in the parish church of Buckingham Palace.

INFORMATION

Tube: Charing Cross
Also for the church
(see p. 52)
☎ 0207 766 1100
Every day 8am-5pm
Free concerts at noon
Mon.-Fri.
Entry fee evenings

British Museum

This museum owes its origins to an initiative by Parliament. To finance the purchase of the collection from Dr Hans Sloane, a public subscription was organized. Legacies were then added, as were contributions from travelers and explorers in the 18th and 19th centuries.

Egyptian antiquities

If it were possible to keep only one exhibit, this would have to be the Rosetta Stone, dating from 196 BC and engraved in three languages: hieroglyphic, demotic and Greek. It was this that enabled Champollion to decipher hieroglyphics.

Greek and Roman antiquities

Of note is the representation of the development of ancient Greece across three periods, with the tomb of the Harpies and a section of the frieze from the Parthenon.

Antiquities of the Near East

The riches of the museum are summed up here by the number of acquisitions from western Asia. Under no circumstances should you miss the door to the palace of Khorsabad.

Prehistory and Anglo-Roman antiquities

An item of interest is the Lindow man, a young man aged 25 who died 2,000 years ago and was found in a marsh with his skin still intact.

Medieval antiquities

The treasure of Sutton Hoo is the center point of this period. The objects found in the tomb of an Anglo-Saxon king (a gold belt-buckle, a shield, a sword and some gold pieces) date from the 7th century.

Oriental antiquities

The British Museum was one of the first museums to take an interest in oriental antiquities. Don't miss the sculptures of the stupa of Amaravati.

INFORMATION

Great Russell Street (see p. 64)
Tube: Russell Square
☎ 0207 636 1555
Mon.-Wed. and Sat. 10am-5pm; Thu.-Fri. 10am-8.30pm; Sun. 12-6pm; Closed Dec. 24-26, Jan. 1, Good Friday and May 8. Guided tours: 90 min. Maps available at the entrance

Tower of London

This vast tower on the banks of the Thames served as a royal residence and also as a prison until World War Two. Today transformed into a museum it contains, in addition to a magnificent collection of armaments, the Crown Jewels, famous throughout the entire world.

White Tower

This is the most remarkable of all the towers, with its solid Roman architecture, its four turrets and its impressive dimensions: 35m (115ft) long, 29m (95ft) wide and 27m (89ft) high.

Royal Fusiliers Regimental Museum

This ancient stronghold contains hundreds of knives, firearms, hunting and military weapons as well as one of the most remarkable collections of armor in the world.

Jewel House

Come and admire the Crown Jewels of England: the Black Prince's Ruby, the Koh-i-Noor diamond donated to Queen Victoria by the Company of India, and the Star of Africa, a 530-carat stone mounted on the royal scepter.

Oriental Gallery

This other wing of the barracks houses a collection of arms and other objects from the East and from North Africa, among which is a suit of armor for an elephant!

The Round Wall

This is accessible via Wakefield Tower and from here there are magnificent views over the fortress, the Thames and Tower Bridge.

INFORMATION

Tower Hill (see p. 68)
Tube: Tower Hill
☎ 0207 403 3761
Open Mar-Oct.
Mon.-Sat. 9am-6pm;
Sun. 10am-6pm
Nov.-Feb.
Tue.-Sat. 9am-5pm
Sun.-Mon. 10am-5pm
Disabled access; guided
tours by a yeoman.
Entry fee

St Paul's Cathedral

Located on the high ground of the City of London, during the Roman period this monument was a place of worship dedicated to Diana, the goddess of hunting. The temple was transformed into a cathedral dedicated to St Paul in 604 but was destroyed by fire in 1087. Rebuilt in the 13th century, St Paul's was at that time the largest medieval church in Europe.

The Great Fire of 1666

The Great Fire of London in 1666 got the better of the building. It was to the architect Christopher Wren that the construction of the present cathedral was entrusted in 1675. This was completed in 1708 in the traditional Gothic style of the period.

The dome

The size and shape of the dome has often been compared with St Peter's in Rome: it is 110m (360ft) high and 31m (102ft) in diameter. The brave will need to climb 627 steps to reach the top. There you will have a superb view over the City.

The Whispering Gallery

You can make a stop halfway at the Whispering Gallery. It is so called because of its acoustics. Any whispering near the inner wall can be heard on the other side. And by contrast, any shouts made toward the outside can't be heard at all.

The crypt

The cathedral is known both as a place of ceremony and as a funerary monument. It was here that the national funeral of Winston Churchill took place in 1965 and the marriage of Lady Diana and Prince Charles in 1981. The first burial was that of Wren himself in 1723. Also buried here are Admiral Nelson, the Duke of Wellington, the painter Turner and T.E. Lawrence of Arabia.

INFORMATION

Ludgate Hill (see p. 68)
Tube: St. Paul's
☎ 0207 236 4128
Mon.-Sat. 8:30am-4pm
Gallery and crypt:
Mon.-Sat. 10am-4pm
Entry fee for
these areas

Victoria & Albert Museum

Nicknamed the "V and A" by Londoners, this museum harbors many treasures. Created as the result of an initiative by Prince Albert to collect fine and decorative art, you would need more than a week to cover each of the 145 rooms!

Art and design galleries

Exhibits are displayed in chronological order and by country. The liturgical pieces are most representative of the Middle Ages, with the Eltenberg Reliquary in gilded bronze and ivory, and the Gloucester Candlestick. The Renaissance is represented by the rich collection of Italian sculptures such as the bas-reliefs by Donatello. Thanks to the former colonies, the museum possesses the most important collection of Indian art outside India. Worth seeing for the sake of curiosity is Tipoo's Tiger, a life-sized model reproducing the cries of an English soldier being eaten.

Special collections

The exhibits here are classified by genre. The most notable collections are: musical instruments from the 16th to the 19th centuries and jewelry from 2,000 BC to the present day, including the beautiful Russia crown jewels. The museum also possesses some cartoons produced by Raphael during the execution of his work on the frescoes of the Sistine Chapel.

Henry Cole Wing

This distinct section of the museum houses paintings, engravings, design and photography. Here you will fir works by Constable (notably *Salisbury Cathedral*). Artists such as Turner, Millet and the Dada and pop art movements are also well represented.

INFORMATION

Cromwell Road
(see p. 48)
Tube: South Kensington
☎ 0207 942 2000
Every day 10am-5.45pr
except Dec. 24-26.
Wed. eve. and the last
Fri. of each month
until 8pm
Free entry

Kensington Palace

This former manor house was acquired in 1689 by William III. The monarch entrusted the creation of the palace to Christopher Wren, already the architect of St Paul's Cathedral. It was here that Queen Victoria was born and lived until her coronation. It has subsequently also been the residence of the Princess of Wales and of Princess Margaret, the late sister of Elizabeth II. A section of the palace is open to the public.

20th centuries, with most notably Lady Diana's wedding dress.

The Orangery

After your visit take the opportunity to rest a while at the tearooms. The specialty is orange-scented tea.

The Queen's Gallery

You arrive at the gallery located on the second floor via the superb Queen's Staircase, built in 1690. It has original oak panels. You can visit the former apartments of Queen Mary, wife of William III. Don't forget to view the little 17th-century Dutch paintings that embellish the panels in the dining room.

model as that of the Queen but enlarged in 1696. This will lead you to the antechamber (presence room) and the private room. From here you will go to the King's Gallery where paintings by Van Dyck and Rubens are on display. This direction also leads to the apartments of Queen Victoria, which she shared with her mother, the Duchess of Kent.

The King's Apartments

Here you take the King's Staircase, built on the same

The Court Dress Collection

A rich collection of court dresses from the 18th to the

INFORMATION

On the edge of Kensington Gardens (see p. 67)
Tube: High Street Kensington or Queensway
☎ 0207 376 2858
Every day 10am-6pm (Last entry one hour before) mid-Oct. to mid-Mar., Wed.-Sun.
Entry fee

Tate Britain

Previously known as the Tate Gallery, the museum has been reorganized and now only holds works from the 15th to the 19th centuries. Built on the site of the former Millbank prison, it opened its doors to the public in 1897 thanks to the legacy of its patron Henry Tate. Expect an unusual approach: thematic rather than chronological order. Displayed works change every year since limited space prevents showing everything at once.

English paintings from the 16th to the 19th centuries

This period is shared among three great painters. Hogarth specialized in group portraits with an expressive and even satirical style, as in his picture *The Strode Family*. Gainsborough, who made a happy transition from landscape painting to portraiture, is represented by *Giovanna Bacelli*. More typical of English paintings, landscape art is typified by Constable and his famous picture *Flatford Mill*.

The Pre-Raphaelites

Exclusive to the British, the paintings of this genre take their inspiration from daily life, after the Italian style of the 14th and 15th centuries. *Ophelia* by Millais, and *Proserpine* by Rossetti are the best known. They quickly lost influence to other romantic artists such as Whistler.

The Clore Gallery

Since 1987, an entire wing has been dedicated to Turner. You can follow the evolution of his work thanks to the 300 or so paintings and studies exhibited here. *The Shipwreck, Snowstorm* and *Venetian Countryside* are only a few of the works by this great inspiration to the Impressionists.

INFORMATION

Millbank (see p. 70)
Tube: Pimlico
☎ 0207 887 8008
www.tate.org.uk
Every day 10am-5.50pm except Dec. 24-26.
Free guided tours every day except Sun.
Free entry except to temporary exhibitions

Tate Modern

Since May 2000, those works of art from the 20th century to the present day previously exhibited at the Tate Gallery have been on display in the former Bankside Power Station. It was a gamble which paid off: renovating an industrial building for cultural use. The chimney and the yellow brick walls remain, only a skylight was added in the roof to give better light. The entry via the Turbine Room is impressive.

Still Life/Object/Real Life (Level 3)

These three genres have been gathered together in order to demonstrate their integral role in the evolution of pictorial techniques for depicting daily life. Here you will find Fernand Léger's *Metallic Ballet*, Warhol's *Tin of Campbell Soup* and Duchamp's *Vine leaf*.

Landscape/Matter/Environment (Level 3)

The themes grouped together here allow an appreciation of the changes in the perception of nature from the Impressionists such as Monet (*Poplars on the Epte*), to artists such as Rothko and Dubuffet.

History/Memory/Society (Level 5)

This section of the museum shows the artist's response to the history and events of the 20th century, including Andy Warhol (*Portrait of Jackie*) and the sculpture of Henry Moore.

Nude/Action/Body (Level 5)

Radically differing approaches to the representation of the human form are confronted here. Among the paintings are Bonnard (*The Bath*) and Bacon, and among the sculptures is Giacometti (*Man Pointing*).

INFORMATION

Bankside (see p. 70)
Tube: Southwark, Black-friars; ☎ 0207 887 8008
Mon.-Thu. 10am-6pm
Fri.-Sat. until 10pm
closed Dec. 24-26.
Free entry except for exhibitions

Practicalities

Rooms and location

If you're selecting a hotel for a weekend you should obviously make sure the location is right. You won't have much time to spare and it would be better to stay in the center of London rather than exhaust yourself constantly traveling about. British hotel prices are higher than those on the Continent, but the prices usually apply to the room, not the person. Also be sure to check whether the prices given include tax and service, otherwise the final check might give you a nasty surprise. Breakfast is rarely included, and it is often better to have it elsewhere. On the other hand, there is no need to give tips, except in

the luxury hotels, where it is best to tip the porter. In addition to the selection below, the British tourist office provides a choice of establishments classified according to a system of crowns, which it would be useful to consult before your departure (see p. 7). You can also call the tourist office's reservation service (Accommodation Booking Service) on ☎ 0207 604 2890, which can offer you a wide range of hotels at all price levels. Some hotels have non-smoking rooms.

All the addresses provided in this guide are located in the center of the city and are arranged according to district. It is important to bear in mind that there is a wide range of prices between

hotels and that the price shown is not necessarily an indication of quality.

In order to make a reservation before leaving home – which it is highly recommended that you do – telephone your preferred hotel to make sure that there is a room available on the required date and confirm by email, fax or letter. You may need to leave a deposit by giving your credit card number.

FINDING YOUR WAY AROUND

You will find details of the nearest subway (Tube) station after the address in the Rooms and Food section.

ost all hotels accept both
a International and
erican Express cards.
king a reservation without
redit card could be
icult. Beware of making a
t-minute cancellation, as
ne unscrupulous hotels
l not hesitate to charge
e entire cost of your
cation to your credit card.

nerally speaking, you will
ed to arrive at your hotel
'ore 6pm or your room
aybe given to another
stomer. Of course, if you
e going to arrive late, all
u need to do is to mention
s when making your
servation.

n the day of departure,
ou must leave the room
efore noon, otherwise
ne hotel has the right
o charge you for
nother night.

Restaurants

here are plenty of
estaurants in London that
ill provide you with the
pportunity to sample
uisine from all over the
orld. You really must
ry English cooking,
articularly specialties
uch as *steak and kidney
ie* and *shepherd's pie*, a
amb and vegetable stew

covered with mashed
potatoes. Above all take
advantage of Sunday
lunchtime to sample
*roast beef and Yorkshire
pudding*, a traditional
beef roast accompanied by a
fritter baked in meat
dripping. The English
customarily eat this on
Sunday, and it will be on
the menu of any restaurant
worthy of the name.

London is equally famous
for offering the best Indian
cuisine in the world, with
a wide variety. Don't be
too afraid of the spices,
all the restaurants serve
dishes adapted to sensitive
palates and stomachs.
Another great advantage
of the Indian restaurants
is that they are often very
good value for money.

You won't have to dress
for dinner, unless you are
headed for the most
fashionable restaurants,
most often offering English
or French cuisine.
Service is not always

included in the prices, and
it is usual to leave a tip
amounting to 15 percent
of the check, except in
pubs where this is not
customary. However, do
be careful of credit card
slips left blank in the
hope that you will add
a tip even though it has
already been included.
Not all restaurants will have
a non-smoking area since
this is not obligatory in
Great Britain. It would
be a good idea to inquire
by telephone in advance
if you are troubled by
cigarette smoke. You can
sometimes purchase
cigarettes in a restaurant,
but they will be much more
expensive there than in a
newsagent (tobacco shop).
Finally, don't forget that
the English eat their meals
early, lunch from noon to
2.30pm and dinner from
7pm to 10.30pm.
Outside of these hours it
will be difficult to get served,
and you will have to be
content with a snack or a
fast-food joint.

Hotels

1 - Ruskin Hotel
2 - Fielding
3 - La Gaffe
4 - Edward Lear

☎ 0207 636 34 42
www.etontownhouse.com

Located in three Georgian-style buildings and very close to the University of London, the hotel does not have the soulless décor that its moderate price might lead you to expect. It has a very pleasant garden and a restaurant serving delicious meals.

Ruskin Hotel★

23-24 Montague Street
Tube: Russell Square
or Holborn
☎ 0207 636 73 88
☎ 0207 323 16 62.

This hotel is to be appreciated above all for its perfect location and all its rooms overlook the ea...

Soho

Hazlitt's★★★

6 Frith Street
Tube: Tottenham Court Road
☎ 0207 434 17 71
☎ 0207 439 15 24.

These premises occupy three 18th-century houses at the heart of Soho; it is a popular hotel frequented by artists, with oak-paneled walls decorated all over with little pictures. An amusing detail: Here you can soak yourself in neo-classical bathtubs with feet in the shape of lions' paws.

Bloomsbury

Russell Hotel★★★

Russell Sq.
Tube: Russell Square
☎ 0207 837 64 70
☎ 0207 837 28 57.

Ask for one of the rooms which overlook the gardens of this immense Victorian hotel. It has a very "Old English" interior and ambience.

Academy★★★

17-21 Gower Street
Tube: Goodge Street
☎ 0207 631 41 15

g of the British Museum. A
English breakfast is included
ts very moderate prices (from
) to £84 for a double room),
l in addition there is a
phone in your room. It is very
l kept, under the same
nership for 19 years.

looms Hotel★★★

Montague Street
be: Russell Square
☎ 0207 323 17 17
☎ 0207 636 64 98.

:ated in the literary quarter of
omsbury, the Blooms Hotel
akes it a point of honor to
gularly supply its library with
w books which are loaned to
clients. With only 27 rooms
d a garden opening on the
ighboring British Museum,
s is a very pleasant and
:laxing setting, but quite
pensive (£199 for two).

Bond Street

laridges★★★★

ook Street
be: Bond Street
☎ 0207 629 88 60
☎ 0207 499 22 10.

e line of limousines parked in
ont of its doors and the ladies
hats constantly arriving and
aving like so many living
plicas of the Queen Mother give
u an indication of the palatial
anding of this art-deco building,
managed by staff to match.
laridges is almost an annex of
uckingham Palace, since many
f those closest to the Royal
mily stay here.

South Kensington

Swiss House Hotel★★

71 Old Brompton Road
ube: Gloucester Road
☎ 0207 373 27 69
☎ 0207 373 49 83.

This hotel is different from the
majority of bed and breakfasts. Staff
members are as welcoming as
might be expected from the
attractive plants that climb up the
entrance, and the high-ceilinged
rooms are surprisingly spacious
and very clean. On the other hand
you will be charged a five percent
supplementary fee if you pay by
credit card.

Five Sumner Place★★

5 Sumner Place
Tube: South Kensington
☎ 0207 584 75 86
☎ 0207 823 99 62.

This hotel won the best small
hotel in London prize awarded
by the tourism office in 1991 and
1993. It is located in a very
beautiful Victorian residence,
and breakfast is served in a
conservatory opening onto a very
pretty garden.

Marylebone

La Place★★

17 Nottingham Place
Tube: Baker Street
☎ 0207 486 23 23
☎ 0207 486 43 35
www.hotellaplace.com

La Place is not too expensive for the area (£115): very close to the department stores of Oxford Street and also to Madame Tussaud's waxworks museum. The restaurant of this refurbished hotel offers a rarity: a menu of grills and Swiss cuisine, a sufficiently intriguing combination to tempt you.

The Landmark★★★★

222 Marylebone Road
Tube: Marylebone
☎ 0207 631 80 00
☏ 0207 631 80 80.

A gigantic atrium extending to eight floors connects the rooms of this former headquarters of British Rail, now converted into a hotel. The renovations did nothing to reduce the dimensions of the rooms which are vast. In addition there are a swimming pool, sauna, Turkish bath and gymnasium which the hotel places at your disposal around the clock.

Covent Garden

Fielding★★

4 Broad Court, Bow Street
Tube: Covent Garden
☎ 0207 836 83 05
☏ 0207 497 00 64.

This is one of the rare interesting hotels in the theater district: it opens onto a quiet street lit by 19th-century gas-lamps. It owes its name to Henry Fielding, who practiced at the Bow Street Magistrates Court, in the next street. Both green and flowering plants are to be found in abundance, and there is also an astonishing peculiarity about the rooms: none of them is truly square, and no two are alike. Nor is it very expensive (about £100 for a double room).

Oxford Street

Durrants★★★

George Street; Tube:
Bond St
☎ 0207 935 81 31
☏ 0207 487 35 10.

Established in a former post-house, this hotel has a very good location between Oxford Street and Regent's Park. It has a comfortably sober bachelor atmosphere of leather and wood, and the service is very reasonable. Unfortunately the rooms are quite small.

Edward Lear★★

28-30 Seymour Street
Tube: Marble Arch
☎ 0207 402 54 01
☏ 0207 706 37 66.

This Georgian house has been entirely renovated. Located very near to Oxford Street, it is the former residence of Edward Lear, an 18th-century English humorist. Today, the hotel has two charming little lounges and a dining room (reserved for breakfast). You would be well advised to reserve one of the rooms located at the rear, which are quieter. A good balance between quality and price (£66.50).

Hampstead

La Gaffe★★

107-111 Heath Street
Tube: Hampstead
☎ 0207 435 49 41
☏ 0207 794 75 92.

This hotel, ideally located in the heart of Hampstead but a little far from the center of London, is not excessively expensive. The rooms are not large but they are very nice, and you can also sample the Italian cuisine in the restaurant run by the owners. Please note that all rooms are non-smoking, but there are places inside the hotel where smoking is allowed.

Sloane Square and Knightsbridge

Basil Street★★★

8 Basil Street
Tube: Knightsbridge
☎ 0207 581 33 11
☏ 0207 581 36 93.

This hotel is remarkable since houses one of London's women's clubs, The Parrot Cl As a result, it is mainly wom who stay here. But everyone welcome to appreciate its f furnishings and its pleasa lounges. It is located just behi Harrod's.

Woodville House★★

107 Ebury Street
Tube: Sloane Square
☎ 0207 730 10 48
☏ 0207 730 25 74
www.woodvillehouse.co.

If you like flowers, this Georgia style hotel is for you. Its inter is decorated after the style of Lau Ashley, the rooms are spruce an the four-poster beds are ve inviting for romantic couples.

The Claverley★★★

13-14 Beaufort Gardens
Tube: Knightsbridge
☎ 0207 589 85 41
☏ 0207 584 34 10.

This hotel is the most practic for making several trips Harrod's and for soaking u the local British ambienc From the bathroom to th concierge via the breakfas room, everything here has th hallmark of a luxury woo Coffee, tea and newspapers a freely available.

The Sloane Hotel★★★

29 Draycott Place
Tube: Sloane Square
☎ 0207 581 57 57
☏ 0207 584 13 48.

1 - The Sloane Hotel
2 - Claridges
3 - 22 Jermyn Street

This little hotel is furnished with antiques which you can take away with you if they are to your taste, since the owners, being passionate collectors, sell them in order to buy new ones.

The Willet★★★

42 Sloane Gardens
Tube: Sloane Square
☎ 0207 824 84 15
🖷 0207 730 48 30.

In the pompous Victorian area around Sloane Square, you will appreciate this redbrick hotel. The service is thoughtful and it is a place of discreet luxury. The breakfast here is very good.

Number Eleven★★★★

11, Cadogan Gardens
Tube: Sloane Square
☎ 0207 730 34 26
🖷 0207 730 52 17.

This is one of London's best-kept secrets, since nothing on the outside gives any indication that this is a hotel, and it was also one of the first to be established within a private residence.

Large numbers of celebrities come to enjoy a vacation here amid total anonymity. The lounge with chimney opens onto an attractive winter garden, and the overall atmosphere is one of a luxurious town house with elegant décor and furniture. Among the services available at the hotel is the rental of a Rolls and chauffeur.

Piccadilly

22 Jermyn Street★★★

22 Jermyn Street
Tube: Piccadilly Circus
☎ 0207 734 23 53
🖷 0207 734 07 50.

Fresh flowers in every room, a writing desk much better equipped than with the usual dull postcards and unusable paper and, most of all, one of the best health clubs in the capital. These are the principal qualities of this hotel located in the historic center of London or, to be exact, in the street famous for its custom-made shirts.

Restaurants

1 - Moro
2 - Cru
3 - Bibendum Oyster Bar
4 - Criterion Brasserie

Chelsea

Bibendum Oyster Bar★★★
(Fish)
Michelin House
81 Fulham Road
Tube: South Kensington
☎ 0207 589 14 80.

You must not miss this restaurant located on the first floor of the magnificent Michelin building. Since it does not accept reservations, you will have to stand in line to be seated but it would be better to wait a little while longer to get a seat in the second dining area rather than in the main hall. Preferably, you can finish off with a very good dessert.

Chutney Mary★★★
(Indian)
535 King's Road
Tube: Fulham Broadway
☎ 0207 351 31 13.

The very long menu may alarm you; this is because the best north Indian cuisine which is served here concentrates on dishes that are a blend of influences both Indian and Western. If you can't make up your mind, order selection of dishes to sample which cetainly will not leave you feeling hungry. Otherwise, order lamb with dried apricots, or even order at random – you will not be disappointed.

Sophie's Steakhouse and Bar★★
(Modern English)
311-313 Fulham Road
Tube: Fulham Broadway
☎ 0207 352 00 88
F 0207 349 97 76
Brunch Saturday and Sunday between 11am and 3pm.

In a sandstone room with a great mass of lamps dangling from the ceiling, you can savour

...e of the many wines à la carte ... enjoy a good meal. On the ...enu is a fillet of very lean ...cottish or Irish beef. Fish lovers ...re not forgotten either, there ... salmon steak with dill to be ...ad. The prices are not excessive ...nd the atmosphere is fairly ...laxed.

The City

The Lightship★★
(Modern English)
... A St Katherine's way,
...t Katherine's Docks
...ube: Tower Hill
☎ 0207 481 31 23
📠 0207 702 03 38
...ww.lightshipx.com

...he setting of The Lightship, in ...t Katherine's dock, is totally ...elightful. On the oldest light...hip in the world (dating from ...877), you can sample refined ...uisine. The terrace on the upper ...eck is very pleasant during the ...ummer months. In the hold, ...he cozy atmosphere makes for ... warm and romantic dinner. ...ven though the menu offers ...ts of meat dishes, the salmon ...ricassée with crabmeat and ...ocket is a delight.

Covent Garden

Rules★★
(Traditional English)
...5 Maiden Lane
...ube: Covent Garden
☎ 0207 836 53 14.

...his is the oldest restaurant in ...ondon, founded in 1798. ...lthough the waiters have ...naintained a very traditional ...vay of dressing, the clientele ...10 longer has to be dressed ...n any particular way. From ...ugust onward you can enjoy ...xcellent game, and throughout ...he rest of the year you will ...ind all the English specialties. ...The dessert menu is particularly ...lelicious.

Mayfair

Sofra★★
(Lebanese)
1 St Christopher's Place
Tube: Bond Street
☎ 0207 224 40 80
📠 0207 224 00 22
www.sofra.co.uk

In little St. Christopher's Place, by a pretty fountain, Sofra's terrace is a very pleasant place to eat during the gentle evenings of spring and summer. In this Lebanese restaurant, the diverse mezes (£2.95 each) will certainly appeal to lovers of oriental dishes. With so many little delicacies, you will be able to sample many different flavors for a perfectly reasonable price.

Islington

Upper Street Fish Shop★
324 Upper Street
Tube: Angel
☎ 0207 359 14 01.

You will be surprised to discover that this much-vaunted fish and chip shop looks very much like a French-style bistrot. There is a wide choice and without doubt the best fish soup in the city; very generous portions for a reasonable sum.

Holborn

St John★★
(Traditional English)
26 St John Street
Tube: Farringdon
☎ 0207 251 08 48.

This restaurant offers excellent English cuisine at very reasonable prices. Don't expect a fantastic interior; however, the service is faultless. Try the salted pig's liver, and don't miss out on the pudding, one of the best in the city.

Farringdon

Moro★★★
(Mediterranean Cuisine)
34-36 Exmouth Market
Tube: Farringdon
☎ 0207 833 83 36
📠 0207 833 93 38.

Moro is fashionable in London. Its Iberian dishes have been given awards time and time again by different London guides such as the respected *Time Out*. In a somewhat relaxed décor, the menu draws its inspiration from typically Spanish flavors. The eggplant purée is excellent, especially if accompanied by some caramel-flavored lamb. But note you are advised to make a reservation.

Old Street

Cru★★★
(Modern English)
2-4 Rufus Street
Tube: Old Street
☎ 0207 729 52 52.

In the area around Old Street, you come to Cru as much for its atmosphere as for its dishes or its wine list. In a warm and convivial ambience, a tuna steak with anchovy paste washes down well with a glass of white wine. In addition to all this, the waiters are pleasant, something which never goes amiss. It is preferable to make a reservation to be sure of getting a table.

Great Eastern Dining Room★★

(Asian dishes)
54-56 Great Eastern Street
Tube: Old Street
☎ **0207 613 45 45**
✆ **0207 613 41 37**
**www.greateasterndining.
co.uk**

You could easily spend an entire night at the Great Eastern. In addition to a bar and a nightclub in the basement, it is possible to satisfy your hunger at one of the tables in the restaurant. Two people can eat for around £60, including wine. The menu mixes with some success both Asian and Western dishes. Even though there are often empty tables, it is still better to make a reservation.

Oxford Street

Wagamama

(Japanese)
4 Streatham Street, at the corner of Coptic Street
Tube: Tottenham Court Road
☎ **0207 323 92 23.**

This is a very popular noodle restaurant. Lines are not uncommon but don't be alarmed, the wait will not be long. The soups and the noodles are excellent (£6–£8), many vegetarian, and the whole place is non-smoking.

Piccadilly

Caviar House★★

(Russian and French Cuisine)
161 Piccadilly
Tube: Green Park
☎ **0207 409 04 45**
✆ **0207 493 16 67**
www.caviar-house.com

In a building dating from 1850, this restaurant is split into two parts. At the entrance you can purchase all kinds of vodkas, sometimes at exorbitant prices, and also caviar, including the famous Beluga (£188 for

50g (2oz). Within, a restaurant of Russian appearance awaits the gourmets among you. But make no mistake, the Caviar House provides an excellent example of mainly French cuisine. Moreover, the foie gras fried with mushrooms is first-class.

Criterion Brasserie★★

(Mediterranean Cuisine)
Piccadilly Circus
Tube: Piccadilly Circus
☎ **0207 930 04 88.**

This restaurant belongs to Marco Pierre White, who wanted to make great cuisine available to all. In a magnificent neo-Byzantine interior you will be able to sample this inventive cooking, at affordable prices. The *cappuccino* (chicken soup) is simply divine.

New Mayflower★★

(Chinese)
68-70 Shaftesbury Av.
Tube: Piccadilly Circus
☎ **0207 734 92 07**
Every day 5pm-4am.

In the maze of little rooms that make up this restaurant you can sample very good Cantonese dishes. Don't be afraid to try the most audacious concoctions, such as chicken livers with seafood (calamari, octopus, scallops and shrimps), which are

both a discovery and a real trea‐ Preferably go there in th‐ evening, you can eat there unt‐ very late at night and there wi‐ always be plenty of people.

Mitsukoshi★★★

(Japanese)
Dorland House
14-20 Lower Regent Street
Tube: Piccadilly Circus
☎ **0207 930 03 17.**

You may have some difficult‐ in understanding the menu‐ which is transcribed but quit‐ often not translated; howeve‐ you need only limit yourself t‐ the sashimi, which is one of th‐ best and most varied in the cit‐ The grills are not disappointin‐ either. There is a vast choice o‐ dishes to sample and, i‐ addition, tatamis, a bar an‐ classic wines. Enough to satisf‐ the true connoisseur.

Russell Square

North Sea Fish Restaurant★

(Fish and Chips)
7-8 Leigh Street
Tube: Russell Square
☎ **0207 387 58 92.**

All kinds of fish are available‐ either to be enjoyed sitting at ‐ table or preferably to take ou‐ as the British do. But if you‐ are happy just to see what a fish‐ and chips restaurant is lik‐

1 - New Mayflower
2 - Rules
3 - North Sea Fish
    Restaurant
4 - The Lightship

Soho

Alastair Little★★

(Modern English)
9 Frith Street
Tube: Leicester Square
☎ 0207 734 51 83.

The chef offers a very innovative cuisine, but unfortunately it changes according to the day and the time. It is worth noting that at noon a less expensive option is available in the basement, which could make for a welcome break during day's shopping in this bustling district.

Luxuriance Pekin Cuisine★★

(Chinese)
0 Gerrard Street
Tube: Leicester Square
☎ 0207 734 02 62
☎ 0207 287 35 98.

The Luxuriance Pekin Cuisine is, according English people, one of the best Chinese

without necessarily sampling the specialty, you can try the house vegetable soup.

restaurants in Soho. On checking this out it was found that this reputation was not misplaced. Even if the décor isn't quite glistening, the dishes are excellent. As an entrée, do try the seafood soup (£3.80) before sinking your chopsticks into the Pekin duck with mushrooms (£5.90). It is not possible to walk down Gerrard Street without eating Chinese.

Garlic & Shots★

(Garlic Cuisine)
14 Frith Street
Tube: Leicester Square
☎ 0207 734 95 05
☎ 0207 734 87 22
www.garlicandshots.com

As its name suggests, the specialty of this little restaurant – where you can order right until midnight during the week

and until 1.00am from Thu. through Sat. – is garlic and shots of vodka. The entire menu is garlic-flavored, from the aperitifs (garlic Martini, £2.50) to the dessert (amaretto garlic cheesecake, £3.80), while the cocktail menu comprises more than one hundred different shots (for £15, you can try six)!

Wapping

The Wapping Project★★★

(Modern English)
Wapping Hydraulic Power Station,
Wapping Wall
Tube: Wapping
☎ 0207 680 20 80.

The Wapping is a disconcerting place. In a former hydraulic power station you can sample a very sophisticated and truly diverse cuisine. The restaurant is in partnership with an association of artists and you can often find young talent here. This is one of the London musts, as much unmissable for its dishes as for its décor and its ambience.

Practicalities

Store opening hours

Stores open around 9am for food shopping, an hour later for clothing, homewares and textiles. In general, they close around 6pm with the exception of Thursday, however, when most remain open during the evening, sometimes until 9pm, more often until 7pm. Stores are open throughout the day without a break. Most of the shops in the tourist districts such as Covent Garden are open on Sunday, usually from 12 noon or 1pm until 6pm or 6.30pm. All department stores are closed on Sunday. If you need to buy something special, it would be best to do this on Saturday; the following day you can stroll around with your mind at ease and simple wander into those shops which do happen to be open. Markets are open on Sunday, from early in the morning until about 1pm. On Sunday afternoons you can go to Hampstead, where the two main shopping streets will be busy until the evening.

Making purchases

The majority of chain stores and department stores (Marks & Spencer, John Lewis, etc.) accept international credit cards (American Express, MasterCard, Diner's Club, Visa International). You will usually be required to enter your pin number into the little keypad at the checkout, but sometimes your card will simply be put into the cash till which will then print a small voucher which you wil be asked to sign. You will the be given a copy of the printout. Be careful not to lose your card because anybody could use it. If you ever do lose it or it is stolen, immediately telephone the service center in Great Britain for the appropriate replacement card:

☎ 01604 230 230 (Visa),
☎ 01273 69 69 33 (American Express),
☎ 01252 51 35 00 (Diner's Club),
☎ 0131 42 75 66 90 (Eurocard and MasterCard).

Traveler's checks are very widely accepted if they are in

FINDING YOUR WAY AROUND

You will find details of the nearest subway (Tube) station after the address in the Shopping section.

rling denominations (£);
any other currency you
ll receive an unfavorable
te of exchange.

ices are always displayed in
eat Britain, even in the
ndows. Haggling in the
pres is considered a mark of
ry bad taste, but it will
most be a necessity at the
ea markets where you may
ten be able to save a few
unds.

Delivery and Shipping

you are buying an item of
rniture or other bulky
ject, do not hesitate to have
delivered to you direct.
ou will have to give the
elivery company a copy of
ie receipt, and they will
ve you a packing slip.
l department stores offer
is service, but you could
lso get in touch with a
rivate transportation
ompany. Here are some
ddresses:

restige Freight
adford Business Centre
adford Way, Billericay
☎ 01277 622 223
1on.-Fri. 9am-5pm
his carrier handles parcels
f all sizes and delivers to any
estination in Europe.

he Packing Shop
-12 Pompon Road, SW8
☎ 0207 498 3255
1on.-Fri. 9am-6pm
he Packing Shop specializes
n the packing and trans-
ortation of fragile items.
ts express service even
uarantees delivery within
week.

Lockson Service Ltd
29 Broomfield St.,
London E14
☎ 0208 597 2889
Mon.-Fri. 9am-5pm
This company often deals with
the vendors at the flea market
in Portobello Road. It will
take charge of transporting all
kinds of items, even the Royal
Doulton flowerpot holder that
you have just discovered and
are afraid of breaking. It is
open on Saturday.

Customs

If you come from a member
state of the European Union,
you are not subject to any
customs regulations either
for everyday items or for
antiques and works of art.
In order to cross the border,
all you will need is the
receipt that shows the
name and address of the
supplier, the price paid
before and after tax, the
description of the article
and your name and address.
This document is all you
need whatever the value of
the item you are carrying.
You will not be required
to make any special
declaration. If you are
exporting an item outside
the EU, customs charges
may apply. The shipping
companies listed should be
able to provide advice – ask
before you buy.

Only buy from reputable
vendors, and don't put your
trust in what might look
like a good deal. If you
are buying a work of art,
insist on a certificate of
authenticity, which the
seller is obliged to
provide you with. Generally
speaking a receipt is
necessary. You may be asked
for it by customs and it
could be useful to you if
one day you hope to sell
on what you have just
bought or if you become
the victim of burglary
and need to make a claim
from your insurance
company.

The crème
de la crème

The ultimate in London shopping, nothing is worth missing out on these addresses, the most classic and prestigious of all, to get a glimpse of British good taste. Everything has its price and these stores are expensive but since their products never go out of fashion and are sometimes even guaranteed for life, you will benefit for a long time to come.

Burberry
165 Regent Street
Tube: Piccadilly Circus
☎ 0207 806 13 16
📠 0207 434 26 20
Mon.-Sat. 10am-7pm,
Sun. 12-6pm.

In 1880, Thomas Burberry invented the first waterproof fabric called gabardine, and was soon on the road to fame and fortune. Success is now worldwide, and his distinctive beige checks have come to symbolize pure British style. But beware, fame has a price: In this men's and women's fashion boutique even the accessories such as umbrellas (£89) or scarves (£79) are sometimes out of reach.

Aquascutum
100 Regent Street
Tube: Piccadilly Circus
☎ 0207 675 90 50 / 82 00
Mon.-Sat. 10am-6.30pm
(Thu. 7pm),
Sun. 12-5pm.

Aquascutum has remained a British institution even though it was bought by the Japanese in 1990. The clothing is solid and dependable, the atmosphere more waltz than punk. Men's shirts begin at £40, cashmere sweaters at £295. Ask for the house catalog; you may not want to order anything but it is very attractive.

previously mentioned, you will also find the name of Herbert Johnson. In fact, in the interior of the same store on the right you will find an admirable collection of hats by the dozen, from the most traditional to the most original. This hat designer possesses his own team of stylists who produce their own masculine and feminine designs. A typically English men's cap would cost £45.

waine Adeney riggs

4 St James's Street
ube: Green Park
☎ 0207 629 68 93
lon.-Sat. 10am-6pm.

. no. 54 St. James's Street, ou will find yourself in front f an immense store window ith two bays. Each one has different name over the top. n fact you will find two ssential British brands aside. On the left, the store ffers a very British collection f leisurewear and accessories such as riding saddles, £800 ₀ £1,500). A chic ambience a little formal.

Herbert Johnson

4 St James's Street
ube: Green Park
☎ 0171 408 11 74
₀ 0171 629 31 14
Mon.-Sat. 10am-6pm.
ver the store window

Stephen Jones

36 Great Queen Street
Tube: Covent Garden
☎ 0207 242 07 70
Tue.-Sat. 11am-6pm
(Thu. 7pm).

Considered to be one of the finest milliners in Europe, Stephen Jones designs hats with great originality and

discreet elegance. You can wear any one of his hats without looking as though you had just come from Royal Ascot. They are expensive (£200 for a woman's hat), but for an important occasion this is the place to come.

House of Cashmere

10-11 Burlington Arcade
Tube: Piccadilly Circus
☎ 0207 499 13 49
Mon.-Fri. 9am-5.30pm,
Sat. 9.30am-5.30pm.
The styles are classical and of very good quality, and everything is in cashmere. The prices are high and there will be no courtesy granted unless you look as though you have several Swiss bank accounts.

Berk

6, 20-21 and 46-49
Burlington Arcade
Tube: Piccadilly Circus
☎ 0207 493 00 28
Mon.-Fri. 9am-5.30pm,
Sat. 9.30am-5.30pm.

These two stores occupy a large part of Burlington Arcade; one of them sells very nice Ballantyne sweaters in cashmere or wool. Lots of choice.

MEASURING THE FABRIC YOU NEED

If you wish to buy fabric by the yard/meter at Liberty in order to make a tablecloth, measure the length and breadth of your table without forgetting to add the length of drop you want. For towels, measure those you already possess. If you're making a suit, all the stores will offer to make the calculations themselves, so you won't need to concern yourself with this.

Rigby & Peller

22A Conduit Street
Tube: Oxford Circus
☎ **020 7491 22 00**
Mon.-Sat. 9.30am-6pm,
Thu. 7pm.

Welcome to the very serious official supplier to her gracious majesty the Queen. Their specialty? Custom-made corsets of undoubtedly impeccable quality. If having your waist imprisoned is not your thing, be assured there is also a wide choice of more modern lingerie.

MacKenzie's

169 Piccadilly
Tube: Piccadilly Circus
☎ **0207 495 55 14**
Mon.-Sat. 9.30am-6pm,
Sun. 11am-7.15pm.

Woolens and tartans, very traditional and at the right price: scarves from £8 to £35, V-neck cashmere sweaters at £120.

Joseph

77 Fulham Road
Tube: Sloane Square
☎ **0207 823 95 00**
Mon.-Fri. 10am-6.30pm
(Wed. 7pm), Sat. 10am-
6pm, Sun. 12-5pm.

Joseph is today certainly a recognized designer distributed throughout the entire world. But there is nothing like paying

a visit to the original boutique. In very large and well designed premises, the emphasis is on knitwear of impeccable quality in modern and flowing designs (£150 for a vest), on trousers that are perfectly tailored, etc. The price they pay for success is that the store is often overcrowded.

Browns

18, 23-27, 38, 50 and
62 South Molton Street
Tube: Bond Street
☎ **0207 491 78 33**
Mon.-Sat. 10am-6.30pm
(Thu. 7pm).

All the great designers are brought together in this complex of boutiques spread out along the entire length of the street. Also marked-down designer clothes (see p. 47).

(see p. 47)

Harrod's

87-135 Brompton Road
Tube: Knightsbridge
☎ **0207 730 12 34**
Mon.-Sat. 10am-7pm.

Harrod's isn't just a department store, it is also the most beautiful and the most legendary symbol of compulsive shopping. Even though it offers a very large selection of fashions, it is above all for its tableware, its toys and games and its amazing range of watches on the first floor that you must go there. The Food Hall, an immense selection of foodstuffs in a multicolored ceramic décor (with motifs of fish, game and vegetables, etc.), is a monument absolutely deserving a visit. Be advised that discipline is strict: don't even think of entering with a burger in your hand, be properly dressed carry your backpack in your hand, and note that photographs are not allowed.

Paul Smith

40-44 Floral Street
Tube: Covent Garden
☎ **0207 379 71 33**
Mon.-Fri. 10.30am-6.30pm
(Thu. 7pm), Sat.
10am-6.30pm, Sun.
1pm-5pm.

This cult designer of English male fashion has recently

unched a range for women
a connecting store.
verything is very smart and
egant without being
duced to the conventional,
ad presented on shelves of
ark wood. Take a tour
round the whole place:
ne step to the right as you
ave you will find, at Paul
mith Jeans, both Langley
ourt and his secondary line
ith jeans starting at £70; or
gain, one step to the left,
aul Smith Kids offering,
or example, amusing T-shirts
£35.

he Mulberry House

**1-12 Gees Court,
St Christopher's Place
Tube: Bond Street
☎ 0207 493 25 46
Mon.-Sat. 10am-6pm
Thu. 7pm).**

lothing and accessories in
ashionable leather are the
nain features of this British
ersion of Ralph Lauren.
n a word, fashionable
portswear of good taste
nainly on a hunting theme.
he prices are high for a
evel of quality which can
sometimes be disappointing
yokes of imitation leather
where you were expecting
he real thing).

N Peal

**71 Burlington Arcade
Tube: Piccadilly Circus
☎ 0207 493 09 12
Mon.-Fri. 9am-5.30pm,
Sat. 9.30am-5.30pm.**

The cult address for lovers of
cashmere. These are without
doubt the best in London,
but you will have to pay at
least £200 for a sweater.
Exceptional quality and
an abundance of colors.
This is a priority address to
visit if you want to buy a

sweater or if you are a
connoisseur.

Church's

**133 New Bond Street
Tube: Bond Street
☎ 0207 493 14 74
Mon.-Sat. 9.30am-6pm
(Thu. 7pm).**

Church's shoes have their
ardent supporters, to say
nothing of their fanatics.
Some keep them for more than
20 years, others buy a new
pair every year, while the most
obsessive have several pairs of
the same style. Women can feel
justified in joining in the
obsession since they are less
well provided for outside
London where the choice is
much less wide (see p. 45).
There are also briefcases and
document wallets to treasure
for life.

Westaway
and Westaway

**65 Great Russell Street
Tube: Tottenham Court
Road
☎ 0207 405 44 79
Mon.-Sat. 9.30am-6pm.**

Two addresses next door to
each other, menswear on one side and
womenswear the other.
Woolens of good quality
and very affordable
prices (see p. 65).

Women's
fashions

London fashion has something to offer all women. The most conservative will find the essentials of everyday life, the most fashionable visit the same stores as princesses of royal blood, while the most eccentric can create their own unique look for an evening or a season.

Designers

Katharine Hamnett

202 New North Road
Tube: Angel
☎ 0171 354 44 00
Mon.-Fri. 9am-5.30pm.

Katherine Hamnett is one of the best-known English designers. Without being any less interesting, she caters for all those alarmed by Vivienne Westwood's eccentricity. Take a look at her secondary line, Hamnett Active Collection, her impeccable yet affordable jeans and her clothing for men (jeans £45 to £50, evening dresses from £450).

Marimekko

16-17 St Christopher's Place
Tube: Bond Street
☎ 0207 486 64 54
🖷 0207 486 64 56
Mon.-Sat. 10am-6.30pm,
Thu. 10am-7pm,

Sun. 12-5pm.
www.marimekko.co.uk

At Marimekko you can coordinate your clothes from head to foot without forgetting to accessorize your outfit. This Finnish brand, which has been in existence since 1951, offers pretty blue or red floral full-length dresses (£50) with matching T-shirts (£38). Above all don't forget to cast your eye over the matching tableware and bags.

Caroline Charles

56-57 Beauchamp Place
Tube: Knightsbridge
☎ 0207 589 58 50
Mon.-Sat. 10am-6pm.

Very aristo, this boutique looks more the salon of a private mansion: chimneys, mirrors, etc. Please be sure to take your time. Here you are in the shop of a couturier who designs fashion for princesses, a fact of which the prices will soon convince you (at least £200 for

basic but impeccably
ut skirt). You are in good
ands and you will be very
ell advised.

ast

92 Fulham Road
ube: South Kensington
: 0207 351 50 70
on.-Sat. 10am-6pm,
un. 12-5pm.

his boutique sells original
othing, made by hand,
' Indian and Japanese
ıfluence. It is worth
membering that Great
ritain was once an empire on
global scale. Expect to pay
out £50 to £100 for a dress.

Oasis

92 Regent Street
ube: Oxford Circus
: 0207 323 59 78

Mon.-Sat. 10am-7pm
(Thu. 8pm), Sun. 12-6pm.

Well established among
London fashion, this chain
offers essential designs at very
reasonable prices (leather
jackets £170, dresses and
shirts from £45).

Whistles

12-14 St Christopher's Place
Tube: Bond Street
☎ 0207 487 44 84
Mon.-Sat. 10am-6pm
(Thu. 7pm), Sun. 12-5pm.
Throughout the ten years
that this store has been in

existence, it has continued
to discover new designers
and sell them at ordinary
ready-to-wear prices.
There are several branches
throughout the city (items
from £20 to £1,500).

Malapa

41, Clerkenwell Road
Tube: Farringdon
☎ 0207 490 52 29
Mon.-Fri. 10.30am-7pm,
Sat. 12-5pm.

Enter this little gallery and
discover the designs of the
latest idols of the fashion
world. You can also be the first
to admire the very beautiful
models by the great British
designers of tomorrow. There
is something here to suit
every taste and above all
every pocket.

Tomcat Leather

29 Neal Street
Tube: Covent Garden
☎/🖷 0207 240 18 34
Mon.-Sat. 11am-7pm,
Thu. 11am-7pm30,
Sun. 12-6pm.

Here you are in a paradise of
leather. Even though the
skins come from Italy and
France, all the models have
been created by young
British designers. Here you
can find a man's jacket for
£425 or a woman's coat for
£395. It is also possible to
order custom-made clothes,
but you will have to expect a
two-week wait.

Karen Millen

46 South Molton Street
Tube: Bond Street
☎ 0207 495 52 97
Mon.-Sat. 10am-6.30pm
(Thu. 7.30pm), Sun. 12-6pm.

CLUBWEAR, STREETWEAR, SPORTSWEAR

These newly coined terms represent three of the main
trends in young people's fashion. "Clubwear" is
clothing you wear to the nightclub. This is not at all
about evening dresses, but rather about little satin
skirts in fluorescent colors, 8-inch sequined platform
shoes, etc. "Streetwear" is influenced by what the
skateboarders are wearing, but also by clothing worn
at work (by garbage men, for example), in which case
it is also known as "workwear." Finally, "sportswear"
is the simplest to explain: this is sports clothing which
has been reappropriated for city use.

This brand has several branches in London, and it is without doubt one of the most interesting franchises. The clothes are of good value and just as attractive as those sold by some designers.

APC

40 Ledbury Road
Tube: Notting Hill Gate
☎ 0207 229 49 33
Mon.-Sat. 10.30am-6.30pm,
Sun. 1pm-5pm.

All APC designs are simple and discreet clothes.

Trendy: young and hip

Adhoc

153 King's Road
Tube: Sloane Square
☎ 0207 376 88 29
Mon.-Sat. 10am-6.30pm,
Sun. 12-6pm.

The best place to appreciate real London hysteria: from just looking in the window, you are hooked. The clothes are

absolutely crazy, (fluorescent vinyl, gold, silver, etc.), often provocative, not necessarily in the best taste, but you can find amusing accessories here (such as a pair of pink feathers for £24).

The Common Market

121 King's Road
Tube: Sloane Square
☎ 0207 351 93 61
Mon.-Sat. 10am-7pm,
Sun. 12-6pm.

Don't be put off by the unremarkable name or the plain windows. Inside you will find a vast hall where the creations of the latest and most trendy designers are available. Here you have a veritable supermarket of ready-to-wear items, with G-Star or Diesel jeans starting at £50.

Top Shop

Oxford Circus
Tube: Oxford Circus
☎ 0207 636 77 00
Mon.-Sat. 9am-8pm (Thu. 9pm), Sun. 12-6pm.

Enter one of the largest fashion stores in Europe. Available on four levels are Top Man (for men) and Top Shop brands, as well as all the other fashion designers. All prices and styles are catered for. The accessories section is impressive. There is also a café and a hairstylist.

Apple Tree

62 Neal Street
Tube: Covent garden
☎ 0207 379 59 44

Mon.-Sat. 10.30am-7.30pm,
Sun. 11am-6.30pm.

Occasionally mischievous fashions, with colors both soft and more daring at reasonable prices. You can complete your outfit with some costume jewelry or an updated cowboy hat.

Urban Outfitters

36-38 Kensington High St
Tube: High Street Kensington
☎ 0207 761 10 01
Mon.-Sat. 10am-7pm (Thu. 8pm)
Sun. 12-6pm.

This is the store for 18–30 year olds. It is spacious and you will find a hugh amount of accessories. The first floor is dedicated to house music. On two other floors, very trendy clothes are on display, from all the latest brands.

WOMEN'S EQUIVALENT CLOTHES SIZES

Metric	36	38	40	42	44	46
UK	8	10	12	14	16	18
US	6	8	10	12	14	16

ags

ill Amberg

Chepstow Road
be: Notting Hill Gate
0207 727 35 60
on.-Sat. 10am-6pm
ed. 7pm).

...nce the 1980s, Bill Amberg ...s managed to reach the ...vel of the best among ...ather goods and offers ...riginal collections. The most ...cent designs have been very ...ccessful, in particular the ...Tropez line and also its ...thon-skin bags. Eccentric ...simple, always original, ...ese are the essential

...ccessories for the fashion ...ctims of the season.

ootwear

Manolo Blahnik

...-51 Old Church Street,
ng's Road
ube: Sloane Square
0207 352 38 63
on.-Fri. 10am-5.30pm,
at. 10.30am-5pm.

...efined ladies will be tempted ...re by the most elegant and ...resistible styles there are. ...he prices may not be quite ...e irresistible, since these ...mptations cost on average

Metric	36	37	38	39	40	41	42	43
UK	3	4	5	6	7	8	9	10
US	5	6	7	8	9	10	11	12

Most high-street stores don't stock shoes in half sizes. More upscale stores, on the other hand, such as Church's, do offer half sizes (3.5 or 4.5 for example).

£300, but there is no ban on enjoying oneself.

Deliss

15 St Albans Grove
Tube: Kensington
High Street
☎ 0207 938 22 55
Mon.-Fri. 9.30am-5.30pm,
Sat. 10am-2pm.

Here you can have exceptional shoes custom-made, starting at £450. There is no need to extend your vacation in London for this, they will be sent to you as soon as they are ready.

Patrick Cox

129 Sloane Street
Tube: Sloane Square
☎ 0207 730 88 86
Mon.-Sat. 10am-6pm
(Wed. 7pm), Sun. 11am-
5pm.

The hallmark of original English shoes. It is especially the moccasins (starting from £125) that are worth buying here. You will find them in

all colors, including those with the British flag on the top. Very smart.

Natural Shoe Store

21 Neal Street
Tube: Covent Garden
☎ 0207 836 52 54
Mon.-Tue. 10am-6pm,
Wed.-Sat. 10am-7pm,
Sun. 12-5.30pm.

Typically British. Here you are guaranteed to find shoes manufactured with the utmost regard for the environment. The designs are very plain but very good (starting at £40).

Men's
fashions

There is nothing like a trip to London for putting a touch of class into your wardrobe. Even if dressing like a lord will cost you the price of your latest automobile, you can at least give yourself the airs of a gentleman farmer or of a polo player.

James Lock and Co
6 St James's Street
Tube: Green Park
☎ 0207 930 88 74
Mon.-Fri. 9am-5.30pm,
Sat. 9.30am-5.30pm.

Established in the 18th century, this hat shop is an institution. The first ever bowler (derby) hats came from this address, and they are still sold today (starting from £175). You will find at James Lock all kinds of hats, such as the splendid panamas (starting at £89). A very warm welcome, even if you are not a client (other hats cost around £125-£145).

John Lobb
9 St James's Street
Tube: Green Park
☎ 0207 930 36 64
Mon.-Fri. 9am-5.30pm,
Sat. 9am-4.30pm.

The quintessence of absolute luxury, here you can have yourself an exceptional pair of shoes custom-made for around £1,820 (excluding tax). You will also require a degree of patience, since the manufacture and delivery times tend to be quite long: Allow six months at least before having the best shoes in the world on your feet. A very nice catalog with all the available styles and advice for maintenance; and helpful staff (see p. 43).

Burro
29 Floral Street
Tube: Covent Garden
☎ 0207 240 51 20
Mon. 11am-7pm, Tue.-Sat. 10.30am-7pm,
Sun. 12-5pm.

Burro is a department store of men's fashion, and

collections are regularly
[fea]tured in the Paris fashion
[dis]plays. It has a simple policy:
[th]ere is no brand, designs are
[sob]er and without a logo.
[tro]users start at £90.

[M] Lewin & Sons

[..]6 Jermyn Street
[Tu]be: Piccadilly Circus
[☎] 0207 930 42 91
[M]on.-Sat. 9am-6pm,
[T]hu. 7pm).

[Av]ailable here is an impressive
[co]llection of classical and
[m]odern shirts (starting from
[£2]7) in a vast choice of
[m]aterials, and some five
[hu]ndred ties at truly
[re]asonable prices (hand-
[m]ade ties start at £42).
[He]re you are sure to find
[on]e to suit your taste.

[J]ones

[..]-15 Floral Street
[Tu]be: Covent Garden
[..]0171 240 83 12
[M]on.-Sat. 10am-6.30pm,
[Su]n. 1pm-5pm.

[Fl]oral Street houses the

[Bi]ggest names in men's
[fa]shion and Jones is a
[ve]ritable temple for you, sir.
[Th]is boutique offers an
[ex]ceptional collection of
[de]signer-wear and gathers
[un]der one roof Christophe
[Le]maire, Dries Van Noten,

Westwood, MC Queen, etc. to
name but a few. From the
presentation to the clothing
itself, everything is beautiful
and very tempting. Watch
your wallet!

Andrew's Ties

49-63 Regent Street
Tube: Piccadilly Circus
☎ 0207 439 88 77
Mon.-Sat. 10am-8pm,
Sun. 12-6pm.

At Andrew's Ties, the choice of
a tie is no trivial matter and
quickly becomes an art form.
Amid hundreds of bow ties, silk
pocket handkerchiefs and
other handmade accessories,
one no longer knows quite
where to turn and the advice of
the saleswoman is more than
invaluable. With prices from
£15, the most skeptical will
perhaps change their mind.

Palomino

5 Flask Walk
Tube: Hampstead
☎ 0207 431 91 41
Tue.-Sat. 10.30am-6pm,
Sun. 12-6pm.

Shirts and sweaters both
unassuming and affordable
(sweaters starting at £45),
typical of "Friday wear," the
new trend which allows men
to dispense with their ties
from Friday onward. There
are also many gift ideas,
notably amusing watches
(from £30 to £180).

Gieves & Hawkes

1 Savile Row
Tube: Piccadilly Circus
☎ 0207 434 20 01
Mon.-Thu. 9am-6.30pm,
Fri. 9am-6pm,
Sat. 10am-6pm.

Of all the Savile Row tailors,
this classic among the
classics makes the clothes
in sober styles for several
actors and a good number
of British politicians. The
prices are a little less sober
than the cut (starting at
£650), but it is all custom-
made. After all, it's true that
perfection has no price tag,
isn't it?

Austin Reed

103-113 Regent Street
Tube: Piccadilly Circus
☎ 0207 734 67 89
Mon.-Sat. 10am-7pm
(Thu. 8pm), Sun. 12-6pm.

WAITING TIMES FOR CUSTOM-MADE

Having a pair of shoes, a shirt or a suit made for
oneself takes time: waiting lists at John Lobb are six
months, not including manufacturing time. It takes
several weeks (on average between six and eight) for a
shirt, and between three and six months for a suit. You
need to consider this if you are planning to get married
wearing Gieves & Hawkes. On the other hand, there is
nothing to stop you from placing an order if you are
only in London for a weekend. Preferably telephone the
store to make an appointment before setting out.

This department store, almost entirely devoted to men's fashion, features the principal international labels (Cerrutti, Hugo Boss, etc.) as well as the house's own label (suits around £500). Many other services are available: barber, shoe shine, etc. Customers are offered tea and coffee.

Richard James

29 Savile Row
Tube: Piccadilly Circus
☎ **0207 434 06 05**
Mon.-Fri. 10am-6pm,
(Thu. 7pm),
Sat. 11am-6pm.

This is the most unconventional of all the Savile Row tailors since it will not think twice about making suits in denim or in less usual colors than black or gray (pistachio green, for example). This eccentricity will please those men who wish to appear elegant but without formality.

The Dispensary

8 Newburgh Street
Tube: Oxford Circus
☎ **0207 287 81 45**
Mon.-Sat. 10.30am-6.30pm,
Sun. 12-5pm.

In the heart of the trendy district of Carnaby Street, The Dispensary provides an outlet for young British designers. In

a brightly lit store, you can find clothing of a very original design. Why not let yourself be tempted by a black Barbour-style jacket with a Mao collar for £95? For relaxed evenings, printed shirts of all kinds (£75) would be in better taste.

Size?

33-34 Carnaby Street
Tube: Oxford Circus
☎ **0207 287 40 16**
Mon.-Sat. 10am-8pm,
Sun. 12-6pm.

Increasingly fashionable, worn in the street, at the office or in the evening, "trendy pumps" alias sneakers or tennis shoes, have become a true fashion accessory. At Size?, styles from the 1980s and 90s can be found on two floors side by side with the latest novelties. Here you can buy a model unique to your taste. In the basement are trendy clothes awaiting dedicated followers of streetwear.

Base London Ltd

30 Carnaby Street
Tube: Oxford Circus
☎ **0207 287 28 65**
✆ **0207 287 28 66**
www.baselondon.com
Mon.-Fri. 10am-6pm, Sat.
10am-7pm, Sun. 12-6pm.

At the shopping heart of Carnaby Street, this brightly lit store is designed on two

levels. On the first floor you can find a fairly classic sweater in acrylic, spandex and nylon for £45. On the second floor the sportswear line with its zippered black woolen sweater for £65 will delight the less formal.

Ted Baker

9-10 Floral Street
Tube: Covent Garden

☎ **0207 836 78 08**
www.tedbaker.co.uk
Mon.-Fri. 10am-7pm, Sat.
10am-6.30pm, Sun. 12-5pm

The Ted Baker line is very much in vogue in Britain. In a very pleasant interior with fitting rooms that look like British beach huts, you will find mainly informal clothing, such as multicket khaki trousers for £75 a zippered beige jacket for 20. A stone's throw from oral Street (1-4 Langley urt), another boutique with small childrenswear section ll round off your choice.

he Duffer of t George

4 Shorts Gardens
ube: Covent Garden
☎ 0207 836 37 22
➍ 0207 379 69 85
on.-Sat. 10.30am-7pm,
un. 12-5pm.

n this little two-story outique, the colored clothing set off to good advantage mid completely white walls. n the second floor, the lassically cut shirts evertheless display a light ouch of eccentricity. Here ou can find shirts with sychedelic motifs for £105 nd a vast array of ties to natch them. For more relaxed veekends, pay a visit to no. 29 cross the street.

Tricker's

7 Jermyn Street
Tube: Green Park
☎ 0207 930 63 95
➍ 0207 930 31 61
www.trickers.com
Mon.-Fri. 9.30am-6pm,
Sat. 9.30am-5.30pm.

Tricker's is an English nstitution in the area of hand-nade leather shoes. This little ll-wood boutique has been

established since 1829. It also has the honor of being one of the official suppliers to HRH the Prince of Wales. But beware, there is a price to pay for this technical expertise, and a pair of moccasins or ankle boots will cost you £215.

Cecil Gee

44-46 King's Road
Tube: Sloane Square
☎ 020 7589 8269
www.cecilgee.co.uk
Mon.-Fri. 10am-7pm,
Thu. 10am-8pm,
Sat. 9.30am-6.30pm,
Sun. 12-6pm.

Cecil Gee is a chain of stores to be found just about everywhere in London. Here you will find all the major Italian brands and the great Japanese designers. It would be easy to let yourself be tempted by a printed black Versace T-shirt or a very up-to-date white Étienne Ozeki shirt with handwritten inscriptions. Be careful all the same when it comes to the prices, they can appear exorbitant.

Reiss

172 Regent Street
Tube: Piccadilly Circus
☎/✆ 0207 439 49 07
www.reiss.co.uk
Mon.-Sat. 10am-7pm, Thu.
10am-7pm, Sun. 12-6pm.

On two floors, Reiss is a trendy brand widespread throughout Britain and across the world. Amid the large marble walls and against a background of techno music, you will find a mixture of a classic look with a somewhat more informal

one. The linen shirt and trousers ensemble, all for £158, is very pleasant to wear on hot summer days.

Lipman & Son's

4 Staple Inn
Tube: Holborn
☎ 0207 404 50 80
Mon.-Fri. 9am-6pm.

Lipman's & Sons upholds the tradition of British class. This shop specializes in typically British suits (between £250 and £300) and top hats. Also available is a very large choice of cuff links, ties and bow ties. Furthermore you may also rent a tuxedo for one of those famous London garden parties.

EQUIVALENT SIZES FOR MEN'S SHIRTS

Metric	38	39	40	41	42	43
Inches	14.5	15	15.5	16	16.5	17

For children

It's now or never – swing into action, realize your fantasies and dress your little golden-haired cherubs as heirs to the Crown. For school uniforms Marks & Spencer may remain the best for quality and value, but many other addresses will provide you with smock dresses and sailor suits.

Buckle My Shoe
18-19 St Christopher's Place
Tube: Bond Street
☎ 0207 935 55 89
Mon.-Sat. 10am-6pm
(Thu. 7pm).

This is the best address in London for children's shoes, stylish and fashionable. It offers exclusively its own designs (from £36 to £55).

Baby Gap
35 High Street, Unit 2-3
Tube: Hampstead
☎ 0207 794 91 82
Mon.-Sat. 10am-7pm,
Sun. 11.30am-5.30pm.

Here you can dress your babies and children in adult fashions. The little denim jackets available from three months upward (£20) are irresistible.

Laura Ashley Mother and Child
449-451 Oxford Street
Tube: Marble Arch
☎ 0207 355 13 63
Mon.-Wed. 10am-6.30pm,
Thu. 10am-8pm, Fri.-Sat.
10am-7pm, Sun. 12-6pm.

Here you will find clothes for babies and for young girls (young boys have been rather neglected), in the same style as other Laura Ashley stores, in other words a predominance of small patterns of little flowers in pastel colors. The items are of good quality, as are the products for adults of this famous brand (expect to pay £40 for a young girl's coat).

Young England
47 Elizabeth Street
Tube: Sloane Square
☎ 0207 259 90 03
Mon.-Fri. 10am-5.30pm,
Sat. 10am-3pm.

The smock dresses in this boutique are worn by the young girls of the fashionable area where it is located. The blazers d Bermuda shorts give you e distinct impression that you e buying a uniform for your n on the eve of his return to on. Expensive, evidently: ound £120 for an eight-year-d's dress.

rench Connection

0 King's Road
ube: Sloane square
0207 225 33 02
on.-Sat. 10am-7pm,
un. 12-6pm.

vo birds with one stone: rectly connected to the adult re, the children's department fers a very successful fashion. e style tends toward the assic, even though some odels remain very modern.

rotters

4 King's Road
ube: Sloane Square
0207 259 96 20
on.-Sat. 9am-7pm,
un. 10am-6pm.

is especially if you have your hildren with you that you need visit this address. They can ave their hair cut here without creams or tears, a rocket ill absorb their attention hroughout the ordeal. There is playing area that you will ave trouble tearing them away rom. If on the other hand you ave left them in the care of our mother-in-law, you can oothe your conscience by ringing them back a DVD, a ook or a game, all of which re available at this store.

Oilily

9 Sloane Street
Tube: Knightsbridge
☎ **0207 823 25 05**
Mon.-Sat. 10am-6pm
(Wed. 7pm).

Brightly colored fabrics, magnificent patchwork dresses, denim jackets for your golden-haired ones… in short, a child's dream and an adult's good fortune. But of course all this will cost you dear. Winter dresses, as well as summer, are on sale from between £50 and £70.

Benjamin Pollock's Toy Shop

44 The Market
Tube: Covent Garden
☎ **0207 379 78 66**
Mon.-Sat. 10.30am-6pm,
Sun. 11am-4pm.

You have to climb the stairs in this little boutique to get to its real treasures, which are magnificent puppet theaters, traditional teddy bears and charming dolls. These are toys for nostalgic adults and careful children, but you can also avail

yourself of whistles, marbles and little figurines, all very pretty and all at a very modest price.

Daisy and Tom

181 King's Road
Tube: Sloane Square
☎ **0207 352 50 00**
Mon.-Fri. 9.30am-6pm
(Thu. 7pm), Sat. 10am-7pm,
Sun. 11am-5pm.

Bring your children here; this place contains a magnificent merry-go-round of wooden horses, a very good bookstore with a soda bar where your little devils can quench their thirst, as well as beautiful toys to suit all pockets, in traditional wood or more fashionable ones, such as the latest series of Harry Potter figures (the Lego Hogwarts Express, or the Basilisk which spits out candy rather than fire).

Sizes of children's clothes are sometimes indicated by age (years or months) and sometimes by height (about 140cm/4ft 6in at ten years, for example). In case of doubt, always take the next size up; it's not uncommon for children of ten to wear clothes for a 14-year-old. Even if you find it difficult to resist a pair of Start Rites with double buckles, it is not recommended to buy the shoes in the absence of the child for whom they are intended.

Department stores

You must go and wander around the department stores for a number of reasons: because here you will find in one place just about everything you could hope to take home with you from London, from a souvenir to a cashmere sweater, from tableware to tea, and because nowhere else in the world will you find any as nice. However, do pay attention to the prices which can be higher than in the boutiques and other stores. The sales periods, though they allow you to make substantial savings, are also the most nerve-racking because they attract so many people.

Dickins and Jones

224-244 Regent Street
Tube: Oxford Circus
☎ **0207 734 70 70**
☏ **0207 437 12 54**
www.houseoffraser.co.uk
Mon.-Sat. 10am-7pm, Thu. 10am-8pm, Sun. 12-6pm.

Dickins and Jones is one of the most popular department stores. Less expensive than Selfridges or Harrod's, all five floors are essentially dedicated to women's fashions, with the biggest names in ready-to-wear. You can also visit a level reserved for men, as well as a limited area for young people. In between purchases you could always take a brief gourmet break in the restaurant on the third floor.

Liberty

210-220 Regent Street
Tube: Oxford Circus
☎ **0207 734 12 34**
Mon.-Wed. 10am-6.30pm, Thu. 10am-8pm, Fri.-Sat. 10am-7pm, Sun. 12-6pm.

Everything about this brand speaks of tradition as you will see from its magnificent Tudor-style interior. Not only are its famous floral fabrics available in all forms imaginable, from handkerchiefs (affordable) to settees (outrageously expensive), but you can also buy simple remnants (starting at £30 a meter/£10 a foot). Liberty also offers a magnificent selection of porcelain, including Wedgwood and Waterford. Its very popular sales take place at the end of June.

Fortnum and Mason's

181 Piccadilly
Tube: Piccadilly Circus
☎ **0207 734 80 40**
Mon.-Sat. 10am-6.30pm
Sun. 11am-5pm.

is is an address for
urmets, whether you are
m London or a tourist. The
st in British fine food is to
found here in a very cozy
terior. And there is no
oblem if you feel like taking
break: The tearoom on the
th floor will welcome you for
revitalizing snack (see p.41).

eter Jones

oane Sq.
ube: Sloane Square
0207 730 34 34
on.-Sat. 9.30am-7pm.

ter this department store, go
st the china department, the
ease-resistant clothes and the
erman underwear, and go
to the top floor. From the
aroom you will have one of
e best views of London. Take
is opportunity for a break.

larvey Nichols

09-125 Knightsbridge
ube: Knightsbridge
0207 235 50 00
www.harveynichols.com
Mon.-Sat.10am-7pm
Wed.-Thu.-Fri. 8pm),
Sun. 12-6pm.

his department store is
ntirely devoted to designer
ashions (for men and
vomen). Here you can buy
our Calvin Klein or Dolce
Gabbana underwear (a very
vide choice of these famous
lesigners' lingerie), or a little
ohn Galliano extravagance
at £2,000, if you have a

mind). This is right now the
most up-to-date of London's
department stores.

Marks & Spencer

458 Oxford Street
Tube: Marble Arch
0207 935 79 54
Mon.-Fri. 9am-9pm, Sat.
8.30am-7pm, Sun. 12-6pm.
This store is the London

flagship of the celebrated
chain. In the food section
there are sandwiches, salads
and cottage cheese, Indian
poppadoms, etc. Why not have
a bite to eat cheaply, around
£3 (see p. 66)? There are
plastic knives and forks at the
checkout. The clothes are also
very good.

John Lewis

278-306 Oxford Street
Tube: Oxford Circus
0207 629 77 11
Mon.-Fri. 10am-8pm,
Sat. 9.30am-6pm.
So you have just made a hole
in your Galliano dress (see
above)? No problem: John
Lewis's range of notions will
provide you with everything
you need, from cotton thread
to the fabric for the alterations.
This department store is much
appreciated by Londoners for
its unbeatable prices.

PERSONAL SHOPPING

This service, offered by some department stores, is
designed to help you carry out your shopping effectively.
In some cases, a member of staff will visit you in your
home to make an inventory of your wardrobe. Then she
will help you draw up a list of missing items. Soon
afterward, you will receive at home the required clothes
on approval. This very personalized service can be
streamlined further and with one telephone call you can
arrange to have the garments delivered to your hotel
room to try on. Among those department stores
offering this service are the following:

Harvey Nichols
Information ☎ 0207 235 50 00.
Free personalized advice for men and women,
changing rooms with showers and refreshments.

Selfridges
Fashion consultation by appointment:
Women: ☎ 0207 318 35 36.
Men: ☎ 0207 318 22 23.
Even outside normal store hours, including Sundays,
a Selfridges' consultant, or a member of staff,
is available for interviewing you to find out your
requirements. She will bring you a choice of clothes
to try on anywhere in London, even at night-time.
There is no obligation to buy. Who could ask for more?

House
and home

Taking advantage of your weekend in London to rethink your interior decoration could be an excellent idea, especially for wallpapers and furnishing fabrics. However, be realistic – having tableware or linen sent home will not be too much of a financial burden, but if you want to buy a Chesterfield sofa or a pair of club armchairs, you will pay a much higher price.

The Irish Linen Company

35-36 Burlington Arcade
Tube: Piccadilly Circus
☎ **0207 493 89 49**
Mon.-Fri. 9.30am-5.30pm,
Sat. 10am-4.30pm.

Here you will find the world's most beautiful sheets, but also the longest-lasting, the kind passed on from mother

to daughter. The prices are high (£625 for a full pair of linen sheets, to which you need to add £65 for a pillowcase of the same quality), but in this specialist house of fine linen there is nothing to stop you from only buying a few handkerchiefs (£3.50 to £12). The store itself is worth going to for its retro interior.

Smallbone & Devizes

105-109 Fulham Road
Tube: South Kensington
☎ **0207 581 99 89**

Mon.-Fri. 9am-5.30pm,
Sat. 10am-5pm.

Whether contemporary or traditional furniture for the kitchen or bedroom, or fabrics for the home, everything here is available custom-made or adapted to your needs. Ideal if you wish to redo your apartment in a British style. Prices of a level your would expect in this area. Overseas deliver available.

The Linen Merchant

11 Montpellier Street
Tube: Knightsbridge
☎ **0207 584 36 54**
Mon.-Sat. 9.30am-6pm.

What a selection of fine linen in this lavender-scented boutique! – sheets for sweet dreams (£30 a set for a child's bed), fancy tablecloths (from £40 to £400!). The most demanding can have their monogram embroidered.

Christopher Wray

99 Shaftesbury Av.
Tube: Tottenham Court Road
☎ 0207 836 68 69
Mon.-Sat. 9.30am-6pm
(Thu. 7pm).

Lovers of contemporary lighting will adore the rails holding spotlights shaped like little swallows. Superb replicas of lamps by Charles Rennie Macintosh, the architect of British art nouveau (from £295 to £495).

Room

115-117 Regent's Park Road
Tube: Chalk Farm
☎ 0207 722 66 22
Every day 12-6pm.

This fascinating little boutique is located near the Camden Lock flea market, a goldmine for antique lovers. With its flashy insignia and funny name, you will not be disappointed. Furniture from the 1970s seems to have

been stolen from the set of a James Bond film. Note in particular the white plastic armchair and the yellow cushion which opens like an oyster.

Laura Ashley

7-9 Harriet Street
Tube: Knightsbridge
☎ 0207 235 97 97
Mon.-Sat. 10am-6pm.

You can transform your apartment into an English garden by supplying yourself with wallpapers and fabrics of floral design (naturally) in this branch store totally dedicated to interior decoration, where the prices are very reasonable (starting at £10 per roll).

The Conran Shop

81 Fulham Road
Tube: South Kensington
☎ 0207 589 74 01

Mon.-Fri. 10am-6pm
(Wed.-Thu. 7pm),
Sat. 10am-6.30pm,
Sun. 12-6pm.

Sir Terence Conran was the founder of Habitat before he opened his Conran Shop in London, and then in Paris. Thanks to great designers, buyers traveling all over the world looking for items, and also the creators of the house look, you can transform your interior in a very original way. Expect to pay, for example, £200 for 3-m (10-ft) shelves by the great British designer Ron Ara. The store in Fulham Road, a former Michelin showroom at the beginning of the last century, is worth a special trip in itself.

Cargo Homeshop

245-249 Brompton Road
Tube: South Kensington
☎ 0207 584 76 11

WALLPAPERS

If you are buying wallpaper – or fabric for the house – be sure to bring very precise measurements of the area you want to cover, that is the total width of the walls and the height to the ceiling. Pay close attention to the quality of the paper: If it isn't coated, it will absorb cigarette smoke and dust, and its lifespan will not be longer than five years. Alternatively, try Laura Ashley for their excellent and very practical vinyl wallpapers for the kitchen. Finally, give some thought to borders to go with the paper, and which will give a very British finishing touch to your interior.

Mon.-Sat. 10am-7pm,
Sun. 12-6pm.

On the face of it, this store is
a hardware store selling
brilliantly sparkling utensils.
A yellow colander, purple
plastic salad servers or a
saltshaker with a "cowhide"
pattern will brighten up the
gloomiest-looking kitchen
without making a dent in
the wallet.

One Deko

**11A Commercial Street
Tube: Aldgate East
☎ 0207 375 32 89
🛆 0207 247 43 82
www.onedeko.co.uk
Tue.-Fri. 11am30-6pm,
Sat. 12-5pm,
Sun. 10.30am-5.30pm.**

For lovers of modern interior
design, a brief tour of One
Deko certainly won't be
a waste of time. Here,
psychedelic-shaped room
lighting is to be found
alongside sofas of original
design. For tea time, a teapot
designed by Oliver Hemming
(£57.50) looks extremely
elegant on the wooden coffee

table with glass center for
playing backgammon.

Silverware

Kings of Sheffield

**5 Cavendish Place
Tube: Oxford Circus
☎ 0207 637 98 88
Mon.-Fri. 10am-5.30pm
Sat. 10am-5pm.**

Sheffield is a very famous
British brand of silverware.
It offers very good value for
money. Nearly all its designs
come in three different
quality ranges: two types that
are silver-plated and one that
is solid silver (i.e. sterling
silver or plain silver). For
a silver-plated set of 44 items
of silverware you should
expect to pay about £219
(guaranteed for life, it would
seem) and £300 for the same
set in solid silver.

London Silver Vaults

**53-64 Chancery House,
Chancery Lane
Tube: Chancery Lane
☎ 0207 242 38 44
Mon.-Fri. 9am-5.30pm,
Sat. 9am-1pm.**

Entering the London Silver
Vaults is truly an adventure.
You descend a long and dimly
lit staircase, giving you time
to ask yourself more than
once whether you have come

to the right address, then
you pass through several
strongroom doors and finally
there you are, in the holy of
holies of London silverware.
The best display for small and
inexpensive items (£5) is that
by David Shure, very useful for
little gifts. One of the most
attractive, Feldman, offers
exceptional items for
thousands of pounds.
Amazing is the fact that all
40 displays have walls hung
with the same blue as the
caskets in which their
silverware is exhibited.

James Hardy & Co

**235 Brompton Road
Tube: South Kensington
☎ 0207 586 50 50
Mon.-Sat. 10am-5.30pm.**

The superb window of this
upscale antique dealer displays
bejeweled silverware, nothing
but rare and magnificent
pieces. You can reassure
yourself of the quality as this
trustworthy company has
been established since 1853!

Fortnum & Mason's

**181 Piccadilly
Tube: Piccadilly Circus
☎ 0207 734 80 40
Mon.-Sat. 10am-6.30pm,
Sun. 11am-5pm.**

The silverware department is
in the basement of this
prestigious establishment.
The floor contains silverware,
porcelain and kitchenware,
but nevertheless offers a good
selection. The antique
silverware is worth a special

(12 at 27-cm/11-in diameter and 12 at 20-cm/8-in diameter) will cost between £500 and £1,200 all the same, according to the design.

Reject China Shop

183 Brompton Road
Tube: Knightsbridge
☎ 0207 581 07 39
Mon.-Sat. 9am-6pm
(Wed. 7pm), Sun. 12-6pm.
A very wide selection of tableware (porcelain and crystal) and for the house. The English porcelain is of a fairly reasonable price, but as for the rest it would be better to wait for the sales periods. The store offers a delivery service overseas, which is quite convenient should you be tempted.

...p. But be careful, even if the ...ices do start at £30, they can ... as high as £1,500 for an ... bucket!

...hina and ...orcelain

...homas Goode & Co

...South Audley Street
...be: Green Park
...0207 499 28 23
...on.-Sat. 10am-6pm.
...he great advantage of this ...partment store is that it ...lls all the main brands of ...rcelain and silverware. ...he marble columns of its ...mmense façade give a clue to ...e store's area and reputation. ...erything is expensive (from ...5 to £1,500 for a china ...ate), but no more so than ...nywhere else.

...edgwood

73-174 Piccadilly
...be: Piccadilly Circus
...0207 629 26 14
...on.-Fri. 9am-6pm,
...at. 9.30am-6pm.
...ext to the famous neo-...assically inspired Wedgwood ...lues,'' you will find top-...uality tableware. Nevertheless ...ou must expect to pay £30 for ...25-cm (10-in) diameter plate.

Royal Doulton

167 Piccadilly
Tube: Piccadilly Circus
☎ 0207 493 91 21
Mon.-Sat. 9.30am-6pm.

Lovers of decorative objects must take a look around here: The brand's own porcelain figurines, flowers or people, are among the most celebrated in the world. This store also has the advantage of being much less expensive than its competitor Wedgwood. However, everything is relative because 24 plates

CARE OF YOUR PORCELAIN

Fine china should not be cleaned in the dishwasher. Simply wash them by hand with liquid soap; do not use any other detergent. Do not use them in microwave ovens, especially if your plates have a gold filigree, and do not subject them to sudden changes in temperature. If you have original plates, do not use them for serving either red fruits or vinaigrettes (salads, asparagus, artichokes, etc.). These foods will tarnish the base material of the crockery by penetrating through tiny cracks in the surface.

Antiques

London is unquestionably one of the world's largest centers for the antiques trade, especially on account of the famous auction houses that have been established here for generations. If you know what you are looking for and you are prepared to pay the price for the missing piece in your collection, then you will be in seventh heaven. If not, don't expect to find the bargain of the century; items can be very expensive, especially once you have added on transportation costs.

Admiral Vernon
141-149 Portobello Road
Tube: Notting Hill Gate
☎ 0207 727 52 42
Sat. 5am-5pm.

A little removed from the more touristy streets of Portobello, this elegant boutique attracts connoisseurs and even some professional buyers who come here to hunt for ornaments, fine china, fashion accessories or jewelry, from the 19th to the beginning of the 20th century. Original souvenirs, and prices not too high.

John Jesse
160 Kensington Church St
Tube: Notting Hill Gate
☎ 0207 229 03 12
Mon.-Fri. 10am-5pm,
Sat. 11am-4.30pm.

John Jesse is a specialist in art nouveau. Devotees will find here

a few items of furniture, lots of very attractive silverware and tableware, but also jewelry and posters by Mucha. This store is one of the best of its kind, but no prices are displayed, and the owner can be about as pleasant as a bear with a sore head.

Bond Street Silver Gallery
111-112 New Bond Street
Tube: Bond Street
☎ 0207 493 61 80
Mon.-Fri. 9.30am-5pm.

The three levels and the 17 displays of this antique store are entirely devoted to silverware and jewelry. It is a prestigious address, the prices

high and the staff might
p a few hints to make sure
u understand this.

etro House

Pembridge Road
be: Notting Hill Gate
0207 243 18 63
ery day 10am-8pm.

u need not be afraid to
mmage through the display
es of this bric-à-brac store.
naments, old toys (Dinky
ys, Snoopys, etc.) and table-
re are arranged according to
ce. Most is available for
tween £2 and £500, which
ows you to enjoy hunting
und without feeling guilty.
ere are also some Formica-
vered items of furniture
es, it's back in fashion).

ray's Antique
Market

Davies Street
be: Bond Street
0207 629 70 34
on.-Fri. 10am-6pm.

his store is interesting not
ly for the antiques available,
t also because it has the
culiarity of having a
bterranean river (the
burn) run through it,
side which you can stop
r a bite to eat. Here you will
d mostly silverware and
bleware, but also antiques
m all over the world.

Eskanazi

10 Clifford Street
Tube: Piccadilly Circus
☎ 0207 493 54 64
Mon.-Fri. 9.30am-5.30pm.

Lovers of ivory will hurry to this
store which offers one of the
most beautiful collections of
netsukes in Europe. But do not
expect to find anything for less
than £1,000. When you are in
love, you don't count the cost.

Alfies Antique
Market

13-25 Church Street
Tube: Edgware Road
☎ 0207 723 60 66
Tue.-Sat. 10am-6pm.

Four stories filled with all sorts
of antiques (jewelry, furniture,
lamps, paintings, etc.). This
is one of the best-stocked
boutiques in London. A true
paradise for collectors.

The Map House

54 Beauchamp Place
Tube: Knightsbridge
☎ 0207 589 43 25
Mon.-Fri. 9.45am-5.45pm,
Sat. 10.30am-5pm.

The five exhibition rooms of
this wonderful boutique,
entirely given over to

cartography, allow you to
appreciate the extent of the
former British Empire, with
documents dating back to
the 17th century.

Gallery of Antique
Costume and
Textiles

2 Church Street
Tube: Marylebone
☎ 0207 723 99 81
Mon.-Sat. 10am-5.30pm.

Here there are fabrics
everywhere, on the shelves,
walls, ceiling and on the floor,
in silk, satin, velvet, chenille,
etc. On the floor below there
are costumes from the 1920s
and 1930s. There is opulence
everywhere you look.

TO BUY OR NOT TO BUY?

You only have a little time, not enough to do a tour
of the stores and compare prices; however, you need
to reach a decision quickly. Before making a foolish
mistake, ask yourself some sensible questions:

■ Is this the type of item aimed at tourists that you will
find cheaper three streets down (this applies
particularly to sweaters and tartans)?
■ Are you sure you won't find the same item at home?
■ Are you sure you will get it cheaper here than at
home (a particularly important question if you need
to have it sent over: inquire in advance about
transportation costs)?

Finally, if you do decide to ruin yourself at a stroke, for
a pair of shoes or a silverware set, draw some comfort
from the fact that this will have given you a great deal
of pleasure and that the item you have purchased will
always be associated with fond memories, something
that you cannot put a price tag on.

Food

The British food that has traumatized many overseas visitors: cucumber sandwiches, fluorescent green peas, lamb with mint sauce and "jelly"! It's time to forget this image and take the opportunity to rediscover British cuisine. It is an excellent way to spend your vacation, and you will certainly not be disappointed.

Tesco Metro
21-22 Bedford Street
Tube: Covent Garden
☎ 0207 853 75 00
Mon.-Sat. 8am-midnight,
Sun. 12-6pm.

More than a supermarket, this is a London way of life. For several years now, Tesco has overtaken "Marks and Sparks" (the popular nickname for Marks & Spencer) in the hearts of the British. Here you will find everything for the home, personal care and household cleaning, as well as a very wide and varied range of foodstuffs. Excellent fresh sandwiches (£1.50–£5) and sliced cheeses. Very handy for a bite to eat.

Planet Organic
42 Westbourne Grove
Tube: Bayswater
☎ 0207 221 71 71
Mon.-Sat. 9.30am-8pm,
Sun. 12-6pm.

Imported from the USA, vegetarian supermarkets are beginning to spread all over Europe. This one is a model of its kind, where all the food is guaranteed free from pesticides or food additives. The fruit and vegetables are so perfect they don't look real, and you can revitalize yourself with a ginger and carrot juice at the adjoining bar.

Tea

Algerian Coffee Sho
52 Old Compton Street
Tube: Leicester Square
☎ 0207 437 24 80
Mon.-Sat. 9am-7pm.

Don't be put off by the sign! This little boutique is very popular with Londoners for its teas. In its retro interior, you will find tea flavored wi your favorite fruit as well as a good old Darjeeling or green tea. It opens onto one of the trendiest streets in London.

Whittards
209 Kensington High Stre
Tube: High Street
Kensington
☎ 0207 938 43 44
Mon.-Sat. 10am-7pm,
Sun. 11am-6pm.

This address is one of the 56 branches of Whittards that

u will come across as you lk around. It is only very cently, following a century quiet activity in Chelsea, at the boutique has veloped in this way. e recipe for its success: aditional teas side by side th very popular fruited as (starting at £3.15 r 125g/4oz, packed in a etal canister), and mugs all colors.

. R. Higgins

9 Duke Street
ube: Bond Street
☎ 0207 491 88 19
Mon.-Fri. 8.30am-5.30pm,
at. 10am-5pm.

his very good purveyor of a, ideally located a short istance from Piccadilly ircus, also sells coffee from e best sources. You must xpect to pay a minimum of 8 per pound (lb), in other ords about 500g of coffee.

. Twining and Co

16 Strand
ube: Temple
☎ 0207 353 35 11
Mon.-Fri. 9.30am-4.45pm.

he gilded lion crowning the ntrance is a reminder that his store was opened in this ocation in 1717. Inside you ill find all the teas available

that are sold under this name (starting at £1.15 for 125g/4oz of English Breakfast), but also a museum tracing the history of what has now become an institution.

Whiskey

Bloomsbury Wine Company

3 Bloomsbury Street
Tube: Tottenham Court Road
☎/🖷 0207 436 47 64
Mon.-Fri. 9.30am-5pm.

This store offers a huge selection of whiskeys of all origins. A bottle of 18-year-old Glenmorangie costs £35. Overseas delivery.

Cadenhead's Covent Garden Whisky Shop

3 Russell Street
Tube: Covent Garden
☎ 0207 379 46 40
www.coventgardenwhisky
shop.co.uk
Tue.-Fri. 11am -7pm,
Mon., Sat. 11am-6pm,
Sun. 12-4.30pm.

A very important address: more than two hundred different brands, from all the regions of Scotland, but also a good selection of Irish whiskeys. Single malts start at £21.50.

Cheese

Neal's Yard Dairy

17 Shorts Gardens
Tube: Covent Garden
☎ 0207 645 35 50
Mon.-Sat. 9am-7pm.

The fact that British cheeses other than Cheddar have been newly resurrected is thanks to the passion of the owners of this store (see p. 57). To get you started, samples are available for tasting. Also on sale is bread made by the famous restaurateur, Sally Clarke.

Paxton & Whitfield

93 Jermyn Street
Tube: Piccadilly Circus
☎ 0207 930 02 59
www.cheesemongers.co.uk
Mon.-Fri. 9am-5pm.

This store has been in business since 1797. All along the walls are arrayed cheeses from the whole world, as well as hams and preserves.

DON'T FORGET!

It is not only tea that you have to find room for in your suitcase. Don't forget Marmite (a yeast extract sandwich spread), orange marmalade and lemon curd (a lemon-flavored spread), all of which will be necessary if you want to recreate at home the taste of a real four o'clock tea. Lovers of exotic flavors would be well advised to slip into their baggage a jar of apple, mango or lime chutney (a sweet and spicy condiment), which goes excellently with chicken. Much stronger than French mustard, mustard powder (Colman's Mustard) will appeal to hardened palates. Finally, try something novel: Bring back some British cheese, it travels well.

Markets

London's markets are like so many Ali Baba's caves, bazaars where you are just as likely to find antiques as secondhand clothes, arts and crafts as organic produce. The food markets (British and exotic) are the simplest way to rub shoulders with real Londoners. Above all though, make sure of the opening days and hours before you go.

Berwick Street Market

Berwick and Rupert Street
Tube: Leicester Square
Mon.-Sat. 9am-6pm.

This is one of the rare basic food markets in the West End and here you can buy cheese, fruit and vegetables.

Spitalfields Market

Commercial Street
Tube: Liverpool Street
Fri. and Sun. 9am-3pm.

Spitalfields is an organic market held beneath an enormous structure which also houses a sports center. All produce is guaranteed free from nitrates and pesticides,

and the return to fashion of eco-produce makes for quite a trendy place to be on a Sunday morning.

Leadenhall Market

Whittington Av.
Tube: Bank
Mon.-Fri. 7am-4pm.

The magnificent Victorian structure built by Sir Horace Jones which covers this market still houses some game merchants (the specialty still sold in season since the Middle Ages), a fishmonger and a cheese store, but the clothes stores and souvenir boutiques have gained ground over the food stores. Go there during the week, early in the morning, when City employees can be seen gulping down an espresso over their newspapers.

Brixton Market

Electric Av., Pope's Road
Tube: Brixton

on., Tue., Thu. and Sat.
30am-5.30pm, Wed.
30am-1pm.

his is London's most
soriating market. Here you
ll only find products from
rica or the Caribbean on
le, from where many of
e communities living in
rixton originate. Spices and
antains, to mention only the
est-known produce, tempt the
asser-by rocked by the reggae
rythms blaring from the
usic stores. Lots of very good
lue secondhand clothes. An
xperience not to be missed.

Portobello Road Market

ortobello Road
ube: Notting Hill Gate
at. 7am-5.30pm.

he section devoted to
ntiques is located nearest
ne subway station, among
harming narrow streets that

soon become packed in fine
weather. Beware though, prices
are geared for the tourist trade
and rise even higher during
the season. Further along you
will find secondhand clothes
and gadgets, and there is a
food market during the week.

Jubilee and Apple Market

**Jubilee Hall and The Piazza,
Covent Garden**

**Tube: Covent Garden
Every day 9am-5pm.**

These two markets tend to
attract essentially a tourist
clientele since they are located
at the heart of Covent Garden.
Leave the sweaters alone, they
may not look very expensive
but are of no value either, and
make do with the souvenirs
and gifts.

The Courtyard

**St-Martin-in-the-Fields
Tube: Charring Cross
Mon.-Sat. 11am-6pm,
Sun. 10am-4pm.**

Those most interested in
originality will be very pleased
with this market located not far
from Trafalgar Square, near the
foot of the church of St.-Martin-
in-the-Fields. This is a meeting

place for numerous British
artists and craftspeople. From
here you can bring back an
original souvenir since you
are just as likely to find
jewelry and glass or sculptured
decorative items as unique
designer clothes.

Brick Lane Market

**Brick Lane and vacinity
Tube: Shoreditch
Sun. 6am-1pm.**

Food and bric-à-brac join forces
in this very popular East End
market where only real
Londoners go. This is one of
the Sunday gathering places
for the Indian and Bangladeshi
communities in London: a very
authentic place where you will
meet the city and its inhabitants
far removed from any clichés.

HAGGLING AT MARKETS

At a flea-market stall, it is not always easy to get the
price of an item or a piece of furniture reduced if you
don't approach the purchase in the right way.
A few catchphrases could help you clinch the deal.
Never ask "How much is it?" but inquire "What do
you want for it?," by which it is understood that you
want to haggle. You should be able to secure a
reduction of at least ten percent.

Discount
and secondhand

Like most big capital cities, London is expensive and living here can be considered a luxury. But the British are very resourceful: discount stores and secondhand shops have become essential venues, where everybody goes quite openly. You, too, can be a smart operator: When taking a vacation in London, don't miss out on a tour of these, you will be sure to make some real savings, if not some surprising deals.

Browns Labels for Less
50 South Molton Street
Tube: Bond Street
☎ 0207 491 78 33

Mon.-Sat. 10am-6.30pm (Thu. 7pm).

Collections from previous years by British and international designers (Gigli, Missoni, Comme des Garçons, etc.) sold at 50 percent of their original price. More affordable than in the stores, but still not exactly cheap (between £60 and £100 for a sweater). A good range of men's fashions, something which is quite rare.

TK Maxx
Drumond Center,
Croydon North End, Surrey
Rail station: East or West
Croydon
☎ 0208 686 97 53
Mon.-Fri. 9am-6pm
(Thu. 9pm), Sat. 9am-6pm,
Sun. 11am-5pm.

This department store offers collections from all the great current designers. Armani, Saint Laurent, Calvin Klein, etc. all available at extraordinary prices (£90 for a Nicole Farhi trouser suit). To take advantage of such bargains, you will need to take the train because this store is outside the city center. But its low prices make the trip truly worthwhile.

Paul Smith

23 Avery Row
Tube: Bond Street
☎ 0207 493 12 87
Mon.-Sat. 10am-6pm
(Thu. 7pm).

The designer's discount store, with very big reductions (see p. 47).

Discount Dressing

58 Baker Street
Tube: Baker Street
☎ 0207 486 72 30
Every day 10am-6pm.

This store sells marked-down designer clothes by the biggest European designers at prices 50 to 90 percent below standard prices. It would be difficult under such conditions to find anywhere cheaper but if you do, Discount Dressing will refund your purchase: cheap… and fair!

Modern Age

65 Chalk Farm Road
Tube: Camden Town
☎ 0207 482 37 87
Every day 11am-6pm.

Here you may hire or buy secondhand originals. Attractive coats in good condition, and above all some superb swimsuits from the 1960s.

In Wear

100 Garratt Lane
Rail station: Earlsfield
☎ 0208 871 21 55
Mon.-Sat. 9.30am-5.30pm,
Sun. 11am-4pm.

This brand of ready-to-wear clothing for both men and women is on sale here at particularly low prices: £10 for a man's jacket, for example. What more is there to say?

Nicole Farhi/
French Connection

3 Hancock Road
Tube: Bromley-by-Bow
☎ 0207 399 71 25
Tue.-Wed., Sat. 10am-3pm,
Thu. 11am-6.30pm,
Fri. 10am-5.30pm.

Here you will find former

collections by the designer Nicole Farhi, including items from her secondary line. Also available are the most basic and best-value clothes of the French Connection brand. Everything is on sale at a reduction of at least 50 percent.

Burberry Factory
Shop

29-53 Chatham Place
Bus 22A, 22B, 48, 55,
253, 277
☎ 0208 985 33 44
Mon.-Fri. 11am-6pm,
Sat. 10am-5pm,
Sun. 11am-5pm.

ENGLISH FASHION MAGAZINES

To be really up-to-date, the specialist press offers you the best advice: It is full of ideas and often includes a large number of store addresses. In general terms these can be divided into two groups: classical or traditional, featuring haute couture designers, and trendy, read essentially by the young. The latter genre of magazines also provides information about music and gives tips on "clubbing" (evenings out at nightclubs). Both types often have carefully chosen graphic art. You can purchase the English language edition of *Elle*, or for men there is *Arena*, the only magazine entirely devoted to male fashion. To give yourself the most up-to-date look, and to get to know the addresses where you will find what you need, read *ID*, *The Face* and above all *Dazed and Confused*. Here you will find the most sophisticated and innovative fashion photographs. These three magazines are today the international benchmarks as far as fashions and trends are concerned.

Don't expect to find the famous raincoats at half-price, but nevertheless there are bargains to be had. This famous house only manufactures clothing that never goes out of fashion. This is not exactly a secret location, so expect to see busloads of tourists, but don't panic: There is enough for everybody.

THE ART OF DRESSING IN "WORN" CLOTHES

Buying secondhand clothes, even regular everyday ones, is quite popular in the UK. The development of charity shops – the generic name for these kinds of clothes and oddments stores – was originally a response to economic conditions: A used outfit is cheaper than a new one. In addition, the charity shops are staffed by volunteers and give their profits to charity. Secondhand clothing has also inspired an entire culture, designers use the look when creating new fashions, young people wear their grandparents' clothes to create a worn, casual look. With a bit of imagination and resourcefulness, you can join in the fun!

Secondhand

The Charity Shop

211 Brompton Road
Tube: South Kensington
☎ 0207 581 79 87
Mon.-Sat. 10am-6pm,
Sun. 12-5pm.

This is one of the many charity shops in the capital. It has the advantage of being supplied by the local well-heeled residents, which means it usually sells clothes of very good quality, sometimes even the best brands, for a maximum of £10.

Pop Boutique

6 Monmouth Street
Tube: Covent Garden
☎ 0207 497 52 62
Mon.-Sat. 11am-7pm,
Sun. 12-6pm.

"Pop" as in pop art or pop music, the 1970s are what it's about here. Secondhand clothes but also old stocks, especially jeans (starting at £20) to cobble together a total seventies look. This is one of the favorite addresses of London students, because of its reasonable prices. Here you will also find retro radios starting at £40, and some magnificent toasters.

Poundstretcher

78/102 Broadway
Tube: St James's Park
(not far from Westminster)
☎ 0208 503 1104
Mon.-Sat. 9am-6pm,
Sun. 10.30am-4.30pm.

Poundstretcher is a chain of discount stores widespread throughout Great Britain.

Here you will find everything: clothing for men, women and children, household items, health and beauty aids, chocolates, cakes, and even disguises and decorations for Halloween and all the major holidays.

Sheila Cook

283 Westbourne Grove
Tube: Notting Hill Gate
☎ 0207 792 80 01
Fri. 10am-6pm, Sat.
8am-6pm, Tue.-Thu. by
appointment.

All the clothes in this elegant boutique are carefully selected by its owner, and sold in excellent condition. Nothing but rarities dating from 1760 to 1960, lots of fabrics and accessories. Prices vary from £3 for a

ndkerchief to £3,000 for
ress.

urence Corner

-64 Hampstead Road
be: Warren Street
0207 813 10 10
n.-Sat. 9.30am-6pm.

ns of American surplus will
l lucky here. Whether for
-hirts, military-style jackets
work overalls, prices vary
m £5 to £30. But take your
ne if you want to find a
·gain.

haft

 Camden Road
ibe: Camden Town
0207 916 30 87
on.-Sat. 11am-7pm,
ın. 12-6pm.

 this pleasant and spacious
>re, admittedly a little
moved from the market, you
ll find trendy secondhand
othes at quite good prices.
ummage also in the
verything at £2'' section.
n't miss the T-shirts with
nny slogans.

olly Diamond

 Pembridge Road
ibe: Notting Hill Gate
 0207 792 24 79
lon.-Fri. 10.30am-6.30pm,
at. 9.30am-6.30pm,
un. 12-6pm.

ter having been closed for

more than a year, Dolly
Diamond has opened its doors
again much to the satisfaction
of the London public. From
retro styles to 1980s looks,
here you will find elegant
secondhand clothes of very
good quality. Sequined evening
dresses for £75. If your discovery
needs a little touching up, this
boutique will take care of it.

Rokit

225 Camden High Street
Tube: Camden Town
☎ 0207 267 30 46
Mon.-Fri. 10am-6.30pm,
Sat.-Sun. 10am-7pm.

Most of the boutiques in this
street have polished and
imposing frontages. This store
sells secondhand clothes on
two floors. There is something
here for every taste, from
inexpensive bikinis to dresses
encrusted with faux jewels,
via floral shirts and ties.

Arch 47,
What goes around
comes around

47 Stables Market,
Shalk Farm Road
Tube: Camden Town
☎ 0797 629 90 20
☏ 0207 388 39 68
Sun. 12-6pm.

When entering the Stables
Market, you find yourself in

the discount and second hand
section of Camden market. A
multitude of stores one after
the other all compete as
treasure houses of original
clothing. This one devotes a
particular area to shirts of
the country's soccer teams,
evidently at a price which
defies all competition.

Cornucopia

12, Upper Tachbrook
Street, Pimlico
Tube: Victoria
☎ 0207 828 57 52
Mon.-Sat. 11am-6pm,
Sun. 12.30-6pm.

An enormous choice of
dresses from 1910 to 1960,
not always in very good
condition but certainly at the
lowest prices. You can spend
hours here trying on anything
that appeals to you amid this
pleasant but untidy mess.
You will also find a host of
accessories here.

Designer 2nd Hand
Shop

24 Hampstead High Street
Tube: Hampstead
☎ 0207 431 86 18
Mon.-Sun. 11.30am-6pm.

In this little Hampstead
boutique, many designers'
creations are sold off at very
low prices. They are all in
very good condition.

Gifts

Rather than going to the souvenir stores ("Made in China") located on every street corner, you would do much better to look around the less conventional boutiques where you are sure to uncover that special accessory that more than any other will remind you of your vacation. London has hundreds of original addresses where you will have no trouble finding that amusing, unusual or extravagant souvenir to bring back home.

The English Teddy Bear Company

42 Piccadilly
Tube: Piccadilly Circus
☎ 0207 491 20 91
www.teddy.co.uk
Mon.-Sat. 10am-6pm,
Sun. 12-5pm.

In a store totally devoted to soft toys, young and old alike will find thousands of different teddy bears. On the shelves stacked with bears of every shape and size, you will find Paddington, the darling of all British children. A little

farther along, one of the Queen's guards welcomes you with his soft open arms.

Forbidden Planet

71-75 New Oxford Street
Tube: Tottenham Court Road
☎ 0207 836 41 79
Mon.-Sat. 10am-6pm
(Thu.-Fri. 7pm).

All your favorite heroes are here: X-Files documents, obscure comics, Superman, etc. This boutique specialize in underground comics. Here you will also find all th essential "Wallace and Gromit" merchandise.

Space NK

37 Earlham Street
Tube: Covent Garden
☎ 0207 379 70 30
Mon.-Fri. 10am-7pm
(Thu. 7.30pm), Sun. 12-5pr
Don't be put off by appearances, what you migh

ink is a postconceptual
stallation is actually a
smetics store. Take a look at
ehl's creams (from New
rk, they are discreetly
ckaged), Philosophy (for
eir very humorous names)
d also at the incredible
lors of Antonia's Flowers.

ctopus
Carnaby Street
be: Oxford Circus
0207 287 39 16
on.-Sat. 10am-7pm,
un. 12-6pm.

his boutique is part of a
ain selling original
stume jewelry. If you
e nostalgic for the little
rs of your childhood, you
n acquire a glass collection
their image. Absolutely
sential is the umbrella
th a duck's head.

nder Two Flags
St Christopher's Place
be: Bond Street
/ 0207 935 69 34
ww.undertwoflags.com
e.-Sat. 10.30am-5pm.

r more than 30 years, the
der Two Flags store has
en considered the London
agship for little lead
gurines. Collectors will
joice to find a chess set for
49, or a miniature bobby at

a more affordable price (£45).
Here you can also leaf through
a number of books covering
the different campaigns of the
Napoleonic era.

London Transport Museum Shop
The Piazza
Tube: Covent Garden
☎ 0207 379 63 44
Every day 10am-6pm.

The boutique at the very
interesting transport museum
is fabulous: You won't find
just one but rather a
thousand gift ideas. From the
most kitsch (a porcelain
model of a doubledecker
bus) to the most amazing
(a beautiful photo album of
items found in the subway),
via the most cryptic (a T-shirt
with the phrase "Mind the
gap," which can be heard in
some London subway stations
requiring passengers to be
careful when entering and
exiting the cars). An
inexhaustible goldmine
and not at all expensive.

Penhaligon's
41 Wellington Street
Tube: Covent Garden
☎ 0207 836 21 50 or
8 Cornhill, The Royal
Exchange, EC3
Tube: Bank
☎ 0207 283 07 11
Mon.-Fri. 10am-6pm.

Honor to whom honor is due:
Penhaligon's is the official
perfumer to the Queen. Here
you will find all kinds of very
British perfumes (the best
known, Bluebell, costs £35 for
50ml/1.75fl. oz), sold in
Victorian bottles. Numerous
beauty accessories which make
refined gifts.

Crabtree and Evelyn
239 Regent Street
Tube: Piccadilly Circus
☎ 0207 292 09 70
Mon.-Sat. 10am-6.30pm
(Thu. 8pm), Sun. 12-6pm.
This other typically British
perfumer offers you, in
addition to the classic
fragrances, pot-pourri for
your home, accessories,
teas, porcelains, in short
everything you need if you
are short on ideas for a truly
classical gift to take home
that is inexpensive and in
very good taste.

Jessie Western
82 B, Portobello Road
Tube: Notting Hill Gate
☎ 0207 229 25 44

Mon.- Fri. 10am-6pm, Sat. 9.30am-6pm, Sun. 12-6pm.

In the very colorful neighborhood of Portobello, Jesse Western is one of the most astonishing secondhand stores. In a little boutique in the style of the 19th century with a very confined atmosphere, you can find all sorts of clothes and accessories from the Wild West. Nostalgic collectors of the gold rush will be sure to find superb dresses from the era starting at at £189, or a wizard's wand for £250.

Vinmag Co
247 Camden High Street
Tube: Camden Town
Every day 10am-6pm.

Are you a fan of the movies or of TV series? Pay a visit to this boutique: posters, postcards and T-shirts with the image of your favorite star await you here (£9.99 for a Starsky & Hutch T-shirt).

Faxcessory
Embankment Place,
Villiers Street
Tube: Charing Cross
☎ 0207 321 00 74
Mon.-Fri. 9.30am-6pm,
Sat. 10.30am-5.30pm.

The celebrated Filofaxes, ring-bound personal organizers, make very useful

presents and are a tiny bit snobbish. During your vacation in London, you could save at least 25 percent by comparison with prices in the rest of Europe. There is a vast choice of designs and accessories in this specialty store. For a standard size, leather-covered versions cost £35.

James Smith and Sons
53 New Oxford Street
Tube: Tottenham Court Road
☎ 0207 836 47 31
Mon.-Fri. 9.30am-5.30pm,
Sat. 10am-5.30pm.

"It never rains but it pours" the British say proverbially, and in order to protect yourself against this very London truth you will need to go to Smith and Sons. This venerable institution, located at the same address since 1857, offers custom-made umbrellas and walking sticks. You will have no trouble finding what you are looking for among the impressive choice available, such as this astonishing walking stick with an integral bottle of whiskey (several models, from £40 to £300 according to quality).

Anything Left-handed
57 Brewer Street
Tube: Leicester Square
☎ 0207 437 39 10
Mon.-Fri. 10am-6pm,
Sat. 10am-5.30pm.

Everything for the left-handed in this little Soho boutique: scissors, saucepans, fountain pens and rulers. The store also sells humorous T-shirts and mugs concerning the rights (if one may call them that) of left-handed people.

Scribbler
146 King's Road
Tube: Sloane Square
☎ 0207 584 48 33
Mon.-Sat. 9am-7pm,
Sun. 11am-6pm

In this small King's Road store you will find everything you need to brighten up your correspondence: colored

ationery, fantasy pens as
ll as lots of postcards for
occasions.

gent provocateur

Broadwick Street
be: Leicester Square
0207 439 02 29
on.-Sat. 11am-7pm.

is lingerie boutique opened

Joseph Corre, the son of
vienne Westwood, has in a
ry short time become the
eeting place for women
shion writers. Hurry along
ere. Don't be concerned by
e exterior or think twice
bout shopping inside this is
ot a sex shop. You will find
ry glamorous underwear
om the 1950s as well as
ant-garde creations.

rowler of Soho

7 Brewer Street
be: Leicester Square
0207 734 40 31
Mon.-Fri. 11am-10pm,
at.-Sun. 12-9pm.

oys who are fond of boys
ave a place of honor in this
ery popular boutique. A
ange of fashions where you
ll find a little something to
now-off to Heaven itself the
me evening, books and, a
ttle to one side, videos.
ne of the trendiest places
Soho, where girls are also
ery welcome.

Marks & Spencer

458 Oxford Street
Tube: Marble Arch
0207 935 79 54
Mon.-Fri. 9am-9pm, Sat.
8.30am-8pm, Sun. 12-6pm.

If you don't have much time to
spare, Marks & Spencer is the
ideal place to find lots of little
typically British gifts. There
is a host of suggestions in
the food section: orange
marmalade, Cheddar,
shortbread, and so on.

Sherlock Holmes Memorabilia Company

230 Baker Street
Tube: Baker Street
0207 486 14 26
Mon.-Fri. 9.30am-5.30pm,
Sat. 10am-5pm,
Sun. 11am-4pm.

Lovers of detective novels
are in the right place here.
The hero of Sir Arthur Conan
Doyle is on sale in all his
forms, from quilted teacups
to an amusing game which
will enable you to relive his
adventures.

Equinox – The Astrology Shop

78 Neal Street
Tube: Covent Garden
0207 497 10 01
Every day 11am-7pm.

If the science of celestial
influences is your thing, go
and cast your eye around this
little boutique with its cosmic
ambiance. You will find a

globe or luminous moon for
£15 and a birth chart for £18.

The Tintin Shop

34 Floral Street
Tube: Covent Garden
0207 836 11 31
www.thetintinshop.uk.com
Mon.-Sat. 10am-5.30pm.

This little boutique is the
ideal place if you are a true
fan. Here you will find
everything (key-rings,
briefcases, etc.) with pictures
of the celebrated personalities
created by Hergé.

Penfriend

Bush House Strand
Tube: Temple
0207 836 98 09
Mon.-Fri. 9.30am-5.30pm or
34 Burlington Arcade
Tube: Piccadilly Circus
0207 499 63 37
Mon.-Fri. 9.30am-5.30pm,
Sat. 10am-6pm.

This boutique prides itself on
being the paradise of the
fountain pen, and this is not
an idle boast. All brands
are available, and
everyone will be able
to find the old or new
style pen which
suits their
penmanship
and wallet
best. The
store
also
repairs pens,
and converts
them for the
left-handed.

CARPETS AND RUGS IN TARTAN PATTERNS

If you dream of making your interior over in the style of a
fashionable pub or a British club, this is the address to
go for fabrics for the home and floor coverings in tartan
designs: Chatsworth Carpets, 227 Brompton Road,
0207 584 1386. Here you will find few designs, but
everyone unique: enough to impress your neighbors!
Delivery worldwide.

Practicalities

London is a real paradise for night owls: You will find lots of people in the streets of the city center until 2 or 3am, even until dawn in Soho. Winter makes no difference: the young women still flock to the nightclubs in T-shirts or low-cut dresses. Thanks to Eurostar, some Europeans even go so far as to travel to London to spend Saturday night in the clubs! You may not be a techno Stakhanovite, but all the same treat yourself just this once to something you would never do at home.

Pubs and cafés

There is no problem if you don't feel that you have the energy to go dancing for several hours after spending the whole day walking: The pubs, open from 11am

FINDING YOUR WAY AROUND

You will find details of the nearest subway (Tube) station after the address in the Nightlife section.

to 11pm from Monday to Saturday (10.30pm on Sunday), are very lively, especially on Friday night when Londoners have finished their week's work. Pubs have an important function in Britain; many employees finish their day here. British people don't just go to any pub, but the one in their neighborhood, or their family pub, or the one which supports their favorite soccer or rugby team. If you look carefully, you will notice that some pubs place a poster at

the entrance: "Sorry, no color." This is evidently not a matter of racism, but simply a way of showing that they don't support any particular soccer team.

The atmosphere in the pubs is generally warm, noisy and full of smoke. The regulars will be chattering, often very loudly, about life in the area or commenting on the latest news. Sometimes they will be playing darts as well. There are some pubs, located in the the less affluent areas, that are the

DRESS CODE

Few clubs practice admission by selective entry, although there are some exceptions. Apart from a few chic venues, there is no need to dress up: long dresses and dark ties will be taken at best for a very poor disguise, and at worst you will be refused entry. Eccentricity and clubwear are very much appreciated at the trendiest venues, but this is not the general rule; a simplicity of style will pass for a carefully chosen "no look."

fuge of the unemployed who ave come to squander their elfare money on drink: there no point in lingering, the gulars will very quickly make ou feel unwelcome. You will ot encounter this problem in e center of town, but you ay be surprised to see that any of the customers drink

ithout moderation, even to e point of not being able to and up straight. One of the ost heated moments in the fe of a pub is "last orders:" t 10.45pm a bell will ring remind customers that closing time" is fast pproaching. Everybody then ushes to the bar with great xcitement to buy their final int. However, drinking laws re due to change as this uide went to press. This will robably result in many bars nd pubs staying opening ater and the end of the

"closing time" ritual.

If you are not a beer lover, then be aware that as a matter of course all pubs also sell cider, whiskey and wine. London also has some very good bars, and many of them arrange concerts and shows at weekends. The most fashionable bars are to be found in the center of town: in Soho, Piccadilly and Covent Garden. They are very lively at the beginning of the evening.

Nightclubs

Discos open early, often toward 10pm, and are

already full an hour later. You will pay considerably less if you arrive before 11pm. Don't forget to bring along your student card, if you are still fortunate enough to possess one: Very often it will entitle you to reduced rates. Most discos and nightclubs close at 3am, although some remain open until dawn.

In London there will be about two hundred different evening entertainments each week, and it might seem difficult to find your bearings in this jungle. There is a simple principle involved: Every venue hosts a different organizer each evening. There is therefore no need to go somewhere different for a change of evening or an alternative style of music. Telephone in advance to check or look in *Time Out* which lists all the programs, the types of music and clientele, etc.

SHOWS

If you wish to reserve a ticket for the theater or the ballet, get in touch with the London Tourist Board or the British Travel Centre (see p. 35), or directly with your hotel. You could also always try your luck at the theater kiosk in Leicester Square (see p. 53).

Finally, you can always go direct to the ticket office of the theater or opera house you wish to visit; they are open from 10am to 8pm. There are private ticket agencies established throughout the city, but these will charge a 22 percent commission. Some of them are not very professional, and be particularly wary of those which are located within bureaus de change; these are veritable tourist traps.

Don't expect to be able to reserve an orchestra seat or a seat for a special performance.

It is, however, almost always possible to obtain tickets for the same evening by waiting in line at the front of the venue two hours prior to the performance. Here you may be able to take advantage of any cancellations.

Pubs

1 - Enterprise
2 - The Eagle
3 - Mash
4 - Ye Olde Cheshire Chees

two large terraces are ver
pleasant places to sit and quencl
your thirst in the sun.

Bloomsbury

The Perseverance
63 Lamb's Conduit Street
Tube: Russell Street
☎ 0207 405 82 78.

Here's a pub as traditional
as they come: a subdued
atmosphere, with a warm
wooden interior, where you can
have a drink in peace. But it
is above all for its motley crowd
that it is worth lingering over
your beer here. Notice also the
large chandeliers dangling from
the ceiling.

The City

Dickens Inn
St Katherine's Docks
Tube: Tower Hill
☎ 0207 488 22 08.

In the heart of St. Katherine's
Docks, the Dickens Inn is a retro
pub which has managed to
maintain its typically British
spirit. In the evening, you will
come across businessmen from
the City who come to sip a pint
or two in front of the giant
screen showing live sports
transmissions. In summer, the

Charing Cross

Sherlock Holmes
10 Northumberland Street
Tube: Charing Cross
☎ 0207 930 26 44.

Aside from the beers, this pul
houses a collection of souvenir
connected with the famous
detective, and you can also go and
pay homage in the reconstructior
of Sir Arthur Conan Doyle's office
on the second floor. The autho
used to come here frequently, anc
even quoted it under its forme
name, The Northumberland

ms, in *The Hound of the askervilles*. A very well-known ddress among tourists.

Orange Brewery
7 Pimlico Road
ube: Sloane Square
☎ 0207 730 59 84.

ehind a large bay window you an watch the three local beers, himsically nicknamed the W1, the SW2 and the Pimlico, n the process of fermenting. You an also try them (£2.03 a pint), ney are perfect. One of the best ddresses in the city.

Enterprise
5 Walton Street
Tube: Knightsbridge
☎ 0207 584 31 48.

his is the best place to be for those who on the face of it are alarmed y the popular and infectious tmosphere that gives English pubs heir special charm. Here it is the hampagne rather than the beer hat flows freely, and the T-shirts ave been relegated to the loakroom in favor of shirts and ies. Snobbish? Hardly…

Covent Garden

The Lamb and Flag
33 Rose Street
Tube: Covent Garden
☎ 0207 497 95 04.

Entirely built of wood, and dating from 1627, this is one of the few houses to have survived the Great Fire of 1666. Charles Dickens was in the habit of coming here, and prizefighting has also been practiced. A very pleasant and traditional pub with a long history.

Finsbury

The Eagle
159 Farringdon Road
Tube: Farringdon
☎ 0207 837 13 53.

This is a very popular pub for its good and affordable cooking (£8 on average) as well as for its own brand of beer (the Charles Wells Eagle Bitter, £1.80 a pint) and its wines sold by the glass. It also has the benefit of a small terrace.

Holborn

Ye Olde Cheshire Cheese
145 Fleet Street
Tube: Blackfriars
☎ 0207 353 61 70.

In over 700 years, this pub has survived the Great Fire of 1666 (although it did have to be rebuilt), German bombings during World War Two, and even the relocation of the press during recent years. This is a true historic monument, with sawdust on the floor and little gloomy staircases. It attracts lots of tourists in the evenings.

Princess Louise
208 High Holborn, WC1
Tube: Holborn
☎ 0207 405 88 16.

This has an interior of special historical and architectural interest, including the (Victorian) restroom, and you will love to drink a beer among its decorated columns and its narrow mirrors. The first floor is dark and buzzing with lively conversations, but there is a more peaceful bar on the second floor where you will not be disturbed by the enforced reading of the latest headlines of the *Guardian* or the *Sun*.

Newman Arms
23 Rathbone Street
Tube: Tottenham Court Road; ☎ 0207 636 11 27.

A very small pub, but with some outside tables. The people who come here give it a highly charged and pleasant atmosphere. Don't

be afraid to join them; you will blend right in.

Knightsbridge

Nag's Head
53 Kinnerton Street
Tube: Hyde Park Corner
☎ 0207 235 11 35.

Here you will find a very quiet and almost countrified pub. You can almost forget that you are in the center of London and not in a little village.
The décor is quite traditional, with hunting and piping scenes, but you might be tempted on good days to drink your beer outside in an ocean of greenery.

Soho

Bradleys Spanish Bar
42-44 Hamway Street
Tube: Tottenham Court Road; ☎ 0207 636 03 59.

Take a break from the crowds along Oxford Street and take refuge in this little attractive pub. The owners are pleasant and create one of the most agreeable family atmospheres. The space is quite limited but it does offer intimate corners. Perfect for ending the day.

The French House
49 Dean Street
Tube: Leicester Square
☎ 0207 437 27 99.

This was the reserve headquarters of the French united around General de Gaulle in London during World War Two. Don't be alarmed by the throng of people crowding around this pub. Many customers will in fact be drinking their beer standing on the sidewalk, a very widespread practice when the weather permits. Here you will also find wine on sale. The ambience is very relaxed.

Cafés, bars and discos

1 - Ministry of Sound
2 - Heaven
3 - Grand Central
4 - Comedy Store

Cafés and wine bars

Bloomsbury

The Old Crown

33 New Oxford Street
Tube: Tottenham Court
Road ; ☎ 0207 836 91 21
Mon.- Sat. 10am-11pm.

It's best to come here after the office rush in order to avoid the crowds, and then you can benefit from a comfortable environment with pleasant music, and enjoy a glass in peace.

Mayfair

Hush

8 Lancashire Court
Tube: Oxford Circus
☎ 0207 659 15 00
🖷 0207 659 15 01
www.hush.co.uk
Mon.-Sat.
10am-11pm.

This is one of the most fashionable places in central London. The owner is none other than the son of the actor Roger Moore and you will very often come across celebrities drinking here. Although the exorbitantly priced meals are nothing out of the ordinary, Hush is still a pleasant place to come and enjoy a glass of wine in the evening. Down a paved alleyway, hidden from view, the bar provides a cozy atmosphere on two floors and an outside terrace.

Covent Garden

Saint

8 Great Newport Street
Tube: Leicester Square
☎ 0207 240 15 51
Tue.-Fri. 5pm-2am,
Sat. 7.30pm-3am.

Young techno yuppies, gays or "soon to be models" crowd around this trendy bar. The management very strictly reserves the right of admission, so come with the correct look. Drinks are expensive (£3) but the music is very good. An address for show-offs.

Freuds

198 Shaftesbury Av.
Tube: Covent Garden

☎ 0207 240 99 33
on.-Sat. 10am-11pm,
un. 12-10.30pm.

hose nostalgic for the 1980s
nd the yuppie era will feel very
uch at home in this very sober-
yle bar with its cement interior
nd look of bare metal. Others
ill appreciate it also for its very
uiet ambience and its not-too-
endy artist and student
ientele. Some Sunday evenings
here are jazz concerts.

Café des amis

1-14 Hanover Place
ube: Covent Garden
☎ 0207 379 34 44
Mon.-Sat. 10.30am-11pm.

s the name suggests, you will
ertainly find French wines here,
ut also those from California of
which the English are very fond.
ou can also have a small cheese
aguette snack with your glass
f wine.

Cork and Bottle

4-46 Cranbourn Street
ube: Leicester Square
☎ 0207 734 78 07
Mon.-Sat. 10am-11.30pm,
Sun. 12-10.30pm.

his is one of the best wine bars
n the city, and an ideal corner
n which to recover from your
shopping in one of its little
ranquil alcoves, a glass of
Australian or South African wine
n hand. Staff members are very
helpful.

The Spot

29 Maiden Lane
Tube: Covent Garden
☎ 0207 379 59 00
Mon.-Sat. noon-1am,
Sun. 6pm-1am.

A good place to spend an
evening in a relaxed atmosphere, listening to jazz or soul
music. At weekends this is the
place to observe the mounting
excitement until the hour

approaches that people leave for
the clubs, whether you are a
follower of the crowd or not.
Comedy shows on Mondays.

Oxford Street

Mash

19-21 Great Portland Street
Tube: Oxford Circus
☎ 0207 637 55 55
🖷 0207 637 73 33
Wed.-Sat. 7.30am-2am.

A restaurant by day and a bar by
night, with a retro ambience and
interior typical of 1960s–70s.
With the evening's DJ at the
mixer, you can sample,
surrounded by a middle-class
clientele, any one of the 30
delicious cocktails on offer here,
with prices starting at £6. Why
not try a Mash Passion, made
with a vodka base, passion fruit
and fresh strawberries? Beer
lovers will be delighted with any
one of the house brews.

SAK Bar

49 Greek Street
Tube: Tottenham Court
Road
☎ 0207 439 41 59.

A stone's throw from Soho Square
and located right in the heart of
busy Soho, the SAK Bar is one of
the most fashionable wine bars.
At the end of the afternoon you
can enjoy a glass here in total
peace and quiet while admiring
the exhibition of photographs by
young artists. In the evening,
there is a party atmosphere
among the trendy clientele.

Piccadilly

Comedy Store

1 Oxendon Street
Tube: Piccadilly Circus
☎ 0207 344 02 34
Tue.-Sun. 6.30pm-11pm.
Every day show
8-10.30pm, Fri.-Sat.
midnight-2.30am.

This has been something of a
British comedy institution for
15 years. You can eat here, or
simply drink a beer, and watch
a good-quality show. Clearly,
however, if you are not familiar
with British humor, the jokes
can be somewhat difficult to
follow! A good atmosphere
anyway.

Old Street

Grand Central

93 Great Eastern Street
Tube: Old Street
☎ 0207 613 42 28
www.grandcentral.org.uk
Mon.-Fri. 7.30am-midnight,
Sat. 6pm-midnight,
Sun. 10am-5pm.

When leaving Old Street tube,
the Grand Central will be the
first bar you come across.
Impossible to miss, its décor is
certainly worth casting an
eye over. Immediately behind a
long bar illuminated by
multicolored neon lights there
is is an eye-catching wall of
bottles rising right to the ceiling.
The cocktail list is quite
respectable. What is not so
appealing though is the jazzy
electronic music played so loud
that it is difficult to talk.

Portobello

Beach Blanket Babylon

45 Ledbury Road
Tube: Notting Hill Gate
☎ 0207 229 29 07
Every day 12-11pm
(Sun. 10.30pm).

The unusual interior is worth
a look: an eclectic but
chic mishmash, neo-classical
columns, and an impressive
chimney looking like the
gateway to hell. The clientele is
very varied, but of the yuppie
trend. This bar has a nice lively
atmosphere.

Soho

Bar Italia

22 Frith Street
Tube: Tottenham Court Road
☎ 0207 437 45 20
Mon.-Thu. 7am-5am,
Fri.-Sat. 24 hours,
Sun. 7am-3pm.

You should go to this address after leaving a nightclub, toward 2am or 3am. This is a place where large nubers of revelers congregate since this is the only café open 24 hours a day. The clientele, chatty and smiling even though tired, takes up the entire length of the street with cappuccino in hand. Here you can start up a conversation with anybody about anything, you can experience London as the British do, against a background of kitsch Italian music. A must for its ambience.

The Edge

11 Soho Sq.
Tube: Tottenham Court Road
☎ 0207 439 13 13
Mon.-Sat. 10am-1am,
Sun. 12-10.30pm.

The gazes of the young men dart from corner to corner of this four-story men-only bar (but becoming more and more mixed), one of the preferred locations for London gays. But the cruising is quite subdued, the atmosphere very amicable and relaxed. Quiet during the day, with a summer terrace which overlooks the square, and lively at night.

100 Club

100 Oxford Street
Tube: Tottenham Court Road
☎ 0207 636 09 33
Mon.-Wed. 7.30pm-midnight,
Thu. 8pm-1am, Fri. 8.30pm-3am, Sat. 7.30pm-1am,
Sun. 7.30pm-11.30pm.

A good place for listening to trad jazz, especially fun on Friday nights when the beer circulates around the systems of both the clientele and the jazzmen. Clearly far removed from the time when the Sex Pistols took their first steps on the scene here.

Classic discos

The Cross

King's Cross Goods Yard, York Way
Tube: King's Cross
☎ 0207 837 08 28
Fri.-Sun. 10pm-8am.

It is hard to find this disco hidden away behind railings and a railroad track but you can see this place from a distance attractively covered in ivy. Inside you will be guaranteed the world's best house music in either of the two suites holding almost 450 people. The interior here is cozy, with long red velvet curtains, but also very hot since there is often not much space.

Bar Rumba

36 Shaftesbury Av.
Tube: Piccadilly Circus
☎ 0207 287 27 15
Mon.-Fri. 10am-3.30am,
Sat. 7pm-6am.

Against a background of ac jazz, salsa or house, you ca go and mix with a crowd blasé and trendy nightclubbe who will be here from ear in the evening. The atmosphe is one of an early start: ideal f those who go to bed early.

Jazz Café

5 Parkway
Tube: Camden Town
☎ 0207 916 60 60
Fri.-Sat. 11.30pm-2am (disco); Every day 7pm-midnight for concerts.

In its somewhat cold blue-tint interior there are excellent concer and evening performances for middle-aged audience. Jazz ar acid jazz, sometimes rap, the relaxed for a while. Some of th best concerts in the capital ar given here.

Limelight

136 Shaftesbury Av.
Tube: Leicester Square
☎ 0207 434 05 72
Mon.-Thu. 10pm-3am,
Fri.-Sat. 10pm-3.30am.

Nonbelievers will be overjoye to go dancing in this forme church interior converted int a club. Mainly funk, garag and house music, with a varie clientele.

Cutting-edge discos

Fabric

77A Charterhouse Street
Tube: Farringdon
☎ 0207 336 88 18
www.fabriclondon.com
Fri. 9.30pm-5am,
Sat. 10pm-7am.

This completely new club comprises three immense rooms furnished with the best sound systems. The floor of the "Bodysonic" room is a giant speaker. The music tries to be different and more underground.

1 - Hush
2 - SAK Bar
3 - Café des amis

The Turnmills

3 B Clerkenwell Road
Tube: Farringdon
☎ 0207 250 34 09
www.turnmills.com
Fri.-Sun. 10pm-7.30am.

Not far from the huge Fabric, Turnmills is for listening and swinging to more rhythmic electronic music. But above all you will need to check on programmed events because the visiting DJs are sometimes the best-known on the international scene. Of note are two bars, two dance floors and some small recesses for taking a quiet drink.

Ministry of Sound

103 Gaunt Street
Tube: Elephant & Castle
☎ 0207 378 65 28
Thu. 10.30pm-3am,
Fri. 10.30pm-7am,
Sat. 11pm-9am.

Located in one of the least attractive parts of the city, the Ministry of Sound is the most famous club in London. The fact that other similar places have opened their doors in the last two years makes the atmosphere here a little more bearable. Famous DJs divide the evenings between themselves and offer primarily house and garage music.

Heaven

Underneath the Arches,
Villiers Street
Tube: Charing Cross
☎ 0207 930 20 20
Mon.-Wed. 10.30pm-3am,
Fri.-Sat. 10.30pm-5am.

A magnificent spot, on three floors and a crowd testifying to a success that has not waned in the past 20 years. Heaven remains the gayest address in the city. Parties attended by huge eclectic crowds take place on Thursday and Friday evenings. Not to be missed.

The End

18 West Central Street
Tube: Tottenham Court
Road; ☎ 0207 419 91 99
Mon.-Sun. 9pm.-3am.

Here is a little disco in the center of London where you might like to swing your hips one evening. Lovers of the gloomy and melancholic will soon be inspired by the R 'n' B or electronic sounds. Its originality is that music companies like to promote their artists here. That is why the lines are sometimes very long.

The Fridge

Town Hall Parade,
Brixton Hill
Tube: Brixton
☎ 0207 326 51 00
Mon.-Thu. 10pm-3am,
Fri.-Sat. until 6am.

The main dance floor is dominated by a huge balcony, while the mezzanine level houses a more intimate room. Several bars, plenty of people and a very warm and enjoyable atmosphere. At weekends, the clientele from other clubs generally comes here to end the evening on a more relaxing note.

The Complex

1-5 Parkfield Street,
Islington
Tube: Angel
☎ 0207 288 19 86
Mon., Thu.-Sat. 10.30pm-
4.30am.

Four immense dance halls and a magnificent décor offering diverse music, from funk to breakbeat. Saturday night is the great British garage night. On the top floor, the "Love Lounge" offers a relaxing atmosphere.

Metric Conversion Chart

ote that in the UK both metric and traditional British sizes are in common use.

Women's sizes

Blouses/dresses

U.K.	U.S.A.	Metric
8	6	36
10	8	38
12	10	40
14	12	42
16	14	44
18	16	46

Sweaters

U.K.	U.S.A.	Metric
8	6	44
10	8	46
12	10	48
14	12	50
16	14	52

Shoes

U.K.	U.S.A.	Metric
3	5	36
4	6	37
5	7	38
6	8	39
7	9	40
8	10	41

Men's sizes

Shirts

U.K.	U.S.A.	Metric
14	14	36
$14^{1/2}$	$14^{1/2}$	37
15	15	38
$15^{1/2}$	$15^{1/2}$	39
16	16	41
$16^{1/2}$	$16^{1/2}$	42
17	17	43
$17^{1/2}$	$17^{1/2}$	44
18	18	46

Suits

U.K.	U.S.A.	Metric
36	36	46
38	38	48
40	40	50
42	42	52
44	44	54
46	46	56

Shoes

U.K.	U.S.A.	Metric
6	8	39
7	9	40
8	10	41
9	10.5	42
10	11	43
11	12	44
12	13	45

More useful conversions

1 centimeter	0.39 inches	1 inch	2.54 centimeters
1 meter	1.09 yards	1 yard	0.91 meters
1 kilometer	0.62 miles	1 mile	1. 61 kilometers
1 liter	2.12 (US) pints	1 (US) pint	0.47 liters
1 gram	0.035 ounces	1 ounce	28.35 grams
1 kilogram	2.2 pounds	1 pound	0.45 kilograms

Published by AA Travel Publishing.

First published as Un grand week-end à Londres: © Hachette Livre (Hachette Tourisme), 2004
Written by Sarah de Haro, Catherine Laughton and Fabian Frydman
Maps within the book © Hachette Tourisme

Published by AA Publishing, a trading name of Automobile Association Developments Limited, whose registered office is Fanum House, Basing View, Basingstoke, Hampshire RG21 4EA. Registered number 1878835.

ISBN-10: 0-7495-4837-1
ISBN-13: 978-0-7495-4837-7

English translation © Automobile Association Developments Limited 2006
Translation work by G and W Advertising and Publishing

Cover design by Bookwork Creative Associates, Hampshire
Cover maps © Crown copyright 2005. All rights reserved. Licence number 399221.

Colour separation by Kingsclere Design and Print
Printed and bound in China by Leo Paper Products

Cover credits

Front cover : AA World Travel Library/Max Jourdan; **Back cover** : Partrick Sordoillet (top), L Grandada (bottom)

Picture credits

P. Sordoillet: pp. 2, 3, 11 (ht.r.), 30, 31, 41 (b.g., c.r.), 45 (c.g.), 47 (b.g.), 49 (c.g., c.r.), 55 (ht.g., c.c.), 6 (b.g., ht.r.), 72, 73, 86, 88, 89, 90, 91, 92 (t.l., t.r.), 93, 94, 95 (c.r.), 101 (c.l.), 102 (t.l., b.c.), 103 (b.r.), 10 (b.l.), 105 (b.r.), 106 (t.r.), 108 (t.r., c.r.), 109, 111 (t.r.), 112 (t.l.), 114 (b.l.), 115 (b.l.), 116, 124 (b.l.), 12. (c.l.), 127 (b.c.), 128 (b.c.), 134 (c.l.), 136 (c.l.), 139 (t.l.).
R. Leslie: pp. 10 (t.r., b.r.), 12 (t.l., b.r.), 13 (t.r.), 15 (c.l., t.r.), 22 (t.l., b.r.), 23, 28 (t.r.), 29 (t.r.), 39 (c.c 49 (t.c.), 53 (t.l.), 56, 62 (b.r.), 65 (t.c., b.r.), 67 (t.c., c.r.), 68 (c.r.), 69 (c.r.), 92 (c.c.), 95 (t.r.), 110 (t.l.), 11 (t.l.), 119 (c.l.), 125 (t.r.), 126 (b.r.), 134 (t.l. ; t.r. ; c.r.), 139 (c.r.).
C. Sarramon: pp. 10 (t.l.), 11 (c.l.), 14 (b.r.), 15 (t.l.), 22 (t.r.), 26 (t.r.), 38, 39 (t.l., t.r.), 41 (t.l., t.r.), 43 (t. b.r.), 44, 45 (t.r.), 46 (b.l.), 50, 51 (t.r.), 53 (c.l., t.c.), 54, 55 (b.l.), 57 (c.c., b.), 59 (t.r., b.l.), 60 (c.l., b.r.), 6 (c.r.), 65 (c.l.), 67 (b.l.), 69 (t.c.), 98 (b.c.), 112 (b.r.), 118 (t.r.), 119 (t.r.), 122 (t.r. ; b.c.), 123 (t.r.), 126 (c.l 131 (c.l.).
L. Grandadam: pp. 15 (b.r.), 20 (t.l., t.r.), 21 (c.l., b.r.), 36 (b.r.), 37 (t.l., c.l.), 42, 48, 52, 63 (b.r.), 64, 6 (b.l.), 96, 98 (t.l.), 99 (b.r.), 103 (c.c.), 111 (c.l.), 121 (c.l.), 124 (t.l. ; t.r.)
É. Guillot: pp. 16 (t.l.), 17 (t.c.), 36 (b.l.), 40, 49 (b.c.), 51 (t.l., b.r.), 57 (t.c.), 63 (t.r., c.l.), 70, 71, 92 (c.r. 95 (t.l., c.c.), 99 (t.l.), 100 (t.r.), 101 (t.c.), 103 (t.l.), 104 (t.r.), 107, 113, 114 (t.r.), 115 (t.r.), 118 (b.c.), 12 (c.l.), 130 (c.l.), 131 (t.r.), 132, 134 (c.r.), 139 (t.r.).
L. Parrault: pp. 60 (t.c.), 106 (t.l.), 120 (t.l. ; b.c.), 127 (c.r.).
Peter Tebbit: pp. 66.
Photo Alto: **L. Rozenbaum/F. Cirou**: 18 (t.r., b.c.), 19 (t.c., b.r.).
Elle: **G. Pascal**: pp. 16 (b.r.), 18 (b.c.), 24 (t.l., c.r.), 25 (c.l.), 26 (t.l.), 27 (c.r.), 28 (t.l.), 29 (c.c.), 45 (b.c. 53 (c.r.), 99 (c.c.), 106 (b.r.), 120 (t.r.), 121 (b.r.), 128 (t.l.), 129 (t.r.). **G. Bouchet**: 18 (t.l.), 19 (c.l.), 21 (t.r. 27 (t.l.), 102 (t.r.), 110 (t.r.), 122 (t. l.), 123 (c.l.), 129 (b.c.).
Hachette: pp. 12 (t.r.), 13 (c.l., b.r.), 16 (t.r.), 20 (b.r.), 25 (b.r.), 28 (b.c.), 77 (c.r.).
Ask Images: **A. Eon-Duval**: 32, 74 (c.), 80 (t.r.); **C. Laurent**: pp. 36 (c.r.), 75 (c.l.); **M. Cristofori**: pp. 37 (b.c.), 74 (t.r.), 79 (t.r.), 80 (c.l.), 82 (t.r.), 84 (t.r.) **TRIP**: pp. 76 (t.r.), 78 (t.l.) ; **Marco**: pp. 76 (t.l.) **A. de Gendre**: pp 78 (t.r.) ; **E. Doumic**: pp. ; **TRIP/M. Feeney**: p. 81 (c.r.) **TRIP/M. Lee**: p. 81 (c.l.).
The Sun: p. 10 (b.l.). **I-D**: p. 14 (t.l., t.r,). **Church's**: p. 17 (b.r.), 46 (t.l.), 101 (c.c.,b.r.). **Royal Doulton** pp. 24 (b.r.), 25 (t.r.), 117. **Sanderson**: p. 26 (b.c.). **N Peal**: p. 27 (c.r.). **J. Lobb**: p. 43 (c.l.). **Jigsaw**: p. 4 (b.r.). **DKNY**: p. 46 (t.r., c.r.). **Claridges**: p. 47 (t.r.). **Liberty Textiles**: p. 58, 112 (t.r.). **Muji**: p. 59 (c.r.). **Contemporary Ceramics**: p. 61. **J. Smith & Sons**: p. 65 (c.r.), 130 (t.r. ; b.c.). **Chutney Mary**: p. 11 (c.l.). **Bill Amberg**: p. 105 (c.l.). **Deliss**: p. 105 (t.l.). **Buckle my Shoe**: p. 110 (b.l.). **Benjamin Pollock's** p. 111 (b.c.). **Rj's Honeshop**: p. 115 (c.r.). **Peter Jones**: p. 114 (t.l.). **Space NK**: p. 129 (c.l.). **Penhaligon's** p. 128 (t.r.).
Office de tourisme de Grande-Bretagne: pp. 75 (t.r.), 77 (c.), 79 (c.), 82 (c.l.), 83, 84 (c.). **Agenc Agenda/Tate Modern**: pp. 37 (b.r.), 85.

Illustrations

Pascal Garnier

A02680